#Eternity

#Eternity

— AN LDS GUIDE TO — DATING & MARRIAGE FOR YOUNG ADULTS

#Terry R. Baker, PhD

CFI
An Imprint of Cedar Fort, Inc.
Springville, Utah

ISBN 13: 978-1-4621-1624-9

Published by CFI, an imprint of Cedar Fort, Inc.
2373 W. 700 S., Springville, UT 84663
Distributed by Cedar Fort, Inc., www.cedarfort.com

LIBRARY OF CONGRESS CATALOGING-IN-PUBLICATION DATA

Baker, Terry R., author.
Eternity : an LDS guide to dating and marriage for young adults / Dr. Terry R. Baker.
    pages cm
Includes bibliographical references and index.
ISBN 978-1-4621-1624-9 (alk. paper)
    1. Marriage--Religious aspects--Church of Jesus Christ of Latter-day Saints. 2. Marriage--Religious aspects--Mormon Church. 3. Dating (Social customs)--Religious aspects--Church of Jesus Christ of Latter-day Saints. 4. Dating (Social customs)--Religious aspects--Mormon Church. 5. Christian life--Mormon authors. 6. Church of Jesus Christ of Latter-day Saints--Doctrines. 7. Mormon Church--Doctrines. I. Title.

BX8643.M36B35 2015
248.4'89332--dc23

                            2015007306

Cover design by Shawnda T. Craig
Cover design © 2015 Lyle Mortimer
Edited and typeset by Kevin Haws

Printed in the United States of America

10 9 8 7 6 5 4 3 2 1

Printed on acid-free paper

Praise for

#Eternity

"After teaching dating, courtship, and marriage principles for nearly four decades, Dr. Terry Baker explores the ten timeless principles upon which successful marriages and families are established and maintained as identified in the family proclamation. With a delightful, entertaining pen, this successful Church educator captures your reason and your heart from the first page to the last."

-#Dr. Brenton G. Yorgason, author and biographer

"Many books have been written on marriage. Does the world need another? Probably not, unless you consider this masterful work by Terry Baker. The reader will quickly be engaged by Dr. Baker's crisp and penetrating style, especially his use of insightful analogies and crystal clear explanation of gospel principles relating to marriage. Dr. Terry Baker possesses a wealth of knowledge and practical advice that's now readily available to a spiritually famished world!"

-#Dr. C. Robert Line, author of *Pure Before Thee*

Dedication

This work is dedicated to my wife, Patty, our eight children and their spouses, our ever-expanding posterity, and my precious students for the past forty-five years—whether years ago in seminary or at the institutes adjacent to University of Utah or Brigham Young University. I especially thank my BYU students for their diligence in studying and applying these principles and their many inspired and helpful suggestions in improving this book.

Contents

Preface

This is a book about love that lasts for #eternity. It's about pure love, true love—finding it and perfecting it and using the eternal perspective of the great plan of happiness as the sure foundation to build upon. It's a book about the ideal and challenge given in 3 Nephi 12:48: "Therefore I would that ye should be perfect even as I, or your Father who is in heaven is perfect." The principles reviewed here are helpful for single individuals, dating couples, and married partners alike. These principles can help singles find true love or find peace and contentment, happily married couples stay that way, and troubled couples to find healing and rekindle the fire.

We may think we found true love in our youth and early marriage, only to inevitably find out what happens when children come or leave or when a partner's menopause collides with her mate's midlife crisis. Adjustments must be made along the way when we discover each other's imperfections or else eternal marriages don't last that long.

The ten principles presented in this book will greatly increase the chances of anyone who perfects them to find and keep a love that will last for #eternity. These ten principles should not be ignored or violated if we ever hope to find lasting, true happiness in an intimate relationship.

These ten principles will eventually lead all truth-seekers to perfection. It is *guaranteed* by our creator: "There is a law, irrevocably decreed in heaven before the foundations of this world, upon which all blessings are predicated—and when we obtain any blessing from God, it is by obedience to that law upon which it is predicated" (D&C 130:20–21).

Finding True Love in Perilous Times

The Apostle Paul's description of our times seems extremely accurate today:

> This know also, that in the last days perilous times shall come. For men shall be lovers of their own selves [selfish, self-centered, egotistical], covetous [lustful, jealous, greedy, envious], boasters, proud, blasphemers, disobedient to parents, unthankful, unholy, without natural affection [homosexual, see Romans 1:26–28], trucebreakers [dishonest], false accusers [slanderers], incontinent [Greek for "without self-control"], fierce [violent], despisers of those that are good, traitors [rebellious], heady [Greek for "rash, reckless"], highminded [Greek for "puffed up, conceited"], lovers of pleasures more than lovers of God; having a form of godliness, but denying the power thereof: from such turn away. For of this sort are they which creep into houses, and lead captive silly women laden with sins, led away with divers lusts, ever learning, and never able to come to the knowledge of the truth. (2 Timothy 3:1–7)

What were any of us thinking when we agreed to come to this earth in these last days and try to establish and maintain eternal marriages and families? Satan is good at what he does, and each of the behaviors listed above are genuine relationship killers. Nothing pleases the father of lies more than either stopping eternal marriages from being formed or breaking them up later.

Life in the last days can certainly be perilous, but it can also be greatly satisfying. The Prophet Joseph Smith taught, "Happiness is the object and design of our existence; and will be the end thereof, if we pursue the path that leads to it; and this path is virtue, uprightness, faithfulness, holiness, and keeping all the commandments of God."[1]

I remain optimistic about our chances of overcoming Satan's opposition and passing our final exam, even in these perilous times. In our favor, we live in an age of greater freedom, the fulness of the gospel has been restored, knowledge of the Lord's plan floods the earth, and there are temples throughout most of the world. The kingdom of God is moving forward at an accelerated rate. The true Church continues to gather and develop resources to help provide the promised protection for the righteous in these perilous times (see 1 Nephi 22:17–25). There are so many opportunities available to us and it's absolutely a great time to be here—maybe even the greatest of all times in which to find true love and a fulness of joy. All we have to do is "pursue the path that leads to it" and believe that "the righteous need not fear."

Eternal Perspective Versus Moral Relativism

In over thirty years of reading and writing dating, courtship, and marriage and family literature, I've never found the Brethren nor the scriptures they base their views on to be proven wrong about those. Therefore, this work is written with an eternal perspective that leads us to the type of eternity we want to spend. An eternity governed by the plan of salvation, or the great plan of happiness. It's my experience and assumption that there is a standard upon which we can base truth—the solid rock of scripture and the teachings of modern prophets.

Many people, young and old, in America today believe in what is referred to as moral relativism. This philosophy states there is no absolute truth—that when it comes to questions of moral issues (right and wrong, good and evil), there are no universally objective answers, so anyone's opinion is as valid and good as another's.

If that idea doesn't work in engineering, physics and medicine, why should it work in philosophy, psychology, or even theology? Engineers don't build politically correct bridges, and medical doctors don't ignore the biological differences between men and women.

Because of moral relativism, tolerance has become our nation's supreme virtue. "Who am I to judge?" they say. Tolerance has become more important than truth, and unless we learn that it's our right and, as Latter-day Saints, even our duty to draw firm lines between morally acceptable and morally unacceptable behavior, love and marriages will continue to fail at an alarming rate.

The Ten Best Principles for Finding and Keeping Perfect Love

An eternal perspective starts with the scriptures and the teachings of living prophets. The outline for this book comes from paragraph seven of "The Family: A Proclamation to the World": "Happiness in family life is most likely to be achieved when founded upon the teachings of the Lord Jesus Christ. Successful marriages and families are established and maintained on principles of faith, prayer, repentance, forgiveness, respect, love, compassion, work, and wholesome recreational activities" (*Ensign*, November 1995, 102).

Another source behind the material for this book comes from the love lives of my students over the past forty years. I've heard, in class or in counseling sessions, love stories and relationship frustrations and successes from literally thousands of couples. They taught me a great many correct principles, and I wrote them down over the years.

The Alvin Principle and Summary

There are many single people today who understand this glorious doctrine and diligently seek to fulfill their divine destiny as heirs of God. However, often through no fault of their own, many lack opportunities to fulfill their desires. Over my years of teaching and counseling, I have listened to countless numbers of worthy young adults who were frustrated with their love lives and with the prospect of ever finding eternal mates. The vast majority of these frustrated students over time resolved their search problems, married in the temple, and are actively involved in the process of becoming one with someone who, at times, appears to have been born on another planet. In other words, finding your eternal companion isn't the end of your problems. It's not easy to become one—for a variety of reasons that we will examine in the chapters that follow.

There is comfort in the great plan of happiness for those wishing to marry or to stay married but not yet succeeding, and in the end these wrongs will be righted. Joseph Smith learned an important principle early in his time. I call it the "Alvin principle" or the "he would have if he could have" principle. Joseph's beloved older brother

Alvin died unexpectedly before the Church was restored, meaning before Alvin could be baptized. Later, Joseph was surprised to see Alvin in a vision residing in the celestial kingdom (see Doctrine and Covenants 137:5).

Several Church leaders have spoken about this principle, such as President Lorenzo Snow: "There is no Latter-day Saint who dies after having lived a faithful life who will lose anything because of having failed to do certain things when opportunities were not furnished him or her. In other words, if a young man or a young woman has no opportunity of getting married, and they live faithful lives up to the time of their death, they will have all the blessings, exaltation, and glory that any man or woman will have who had this opportunity and improved it. That is sure and positive."[2]

Also, President Gordon B. Hinckley said, "*Do not give up hope. And do not give up trying. But do give up being obsessed with it. The chances are that if you forget about it and become anxiously engaged in other activities, the prospects will brighten immeasurably.*"[3] Not to mention Elder Neal A. Maxwell's advice: "While we should be 'anxiously engaged,' we need not be hectically engaged. We can be diligent and still do things in 'wisdom and order' without going faster than we 'have strength and means' (Mosiah 4:27; D&C 10:4)."[4]

Our intentions, desires, and seemingly fruitless efforts in seeking or trying to keep an eternal marriage and family will never be in vain in the long run. God—who notices even a sparrow when it falls to the earth (Matthew 10:29–31)—also knows the intentions of our hearts and will take care of all His children who love and obey Him.

The Alvin principle is a true principle that has always been true and will always be true. It's true in all cultures and countries and has been true in all the worlds God has created or will yet create. It's a principle that is true in every circumstance and for every sincere and honest person. There are no exceptions. Happiness for all eternity is a promised blessing for anyone who sincerely seeks it and is willing to follow the path our loving heavenly parents have carefully and clearly laid out, which leads back to them.

Introduction: Living by Gospel Principles

"Happiness in family life is most likely to be achieved when founded upon the teachings of the Lord Jesus Christ."

J oseph Smith once said, "I teach them correct principles, and they govern themselves."[5] Knowing and living by correct relationship principles is essential to finding and keeping eternal love. This book examines one prime principle and nine gospel principles that flow from it and the power they all have to change our lives. These ten principles form a solid foundation for pure love.

The term *relationship principle* here refers to any truth that gives counsel and guidance for conduct in intimate relationships. Correct and true relationship principles can be discovered in a variety of ways, both scientific and spiritual.

Correct principles never change. They are timeless and transcend all cultures. They are lawlike statements that explain the relationship between at least two variables and are general and unspecific in nature. For example, the most basic of all Book of Mormon principles is, "Inasmuch as ye shall keep my commandments ye shall prosper in the land" (2 Nephi 1:20). The independent variable, or the part that we do, is keeping the commandments. The dependent variable, or that which is influenced by our actions, is prospering in the land.

Principles have two parts: *if* and *then*. Religious commandments are different as they only have one part: "thou shalt not." Understanding correct relationship principles that are true in every case gives us the power to make wise decisions in our intimate relationships.

The Prime Principle

We start with the prime principle that the nine other relationship principles depend upon. This principle is clearly stated in paragraph seven of "The Family: A Proclamation to the World," hereafter referred to simply as the family proclamation: "Happiness in family life is most likely to be achieved when founded upon the teachings of the Lord Jesus Christ."

This is one principle that cannot be broken if we expect to find pure love and a fulness of joy for eternity. There can't be any lasting happiness in this life or the next if we try to build our love on any other kind of temporal foundation. That includes extended family relationships, friends, hobbies, employment—anything other than the Savior and His teachings. Jesus Christ is the chief cornerstone of the rock-solid foundation of pure love and marriage. We will examine nine other stones that complete this sure foundation.

All Who Aimlessly Wander Eventually Become Lost

We live in an increasingly secular world that values correct principles and basic truths about right and wrong less and less.[6] I learned years ago that living correct principles concerning marriage relationships is important to all people, not just Latter-day Saints. In the 1980s, I did psychotherapy, marriage, and family counseling at a large counseling clinic in the heart of the Bible Belt. Most of the people I worked with were either inactive members of their churches or had left their churches altogether and become agnostic or atheistic. The majority of the wanderers who came for counseling had decided to abandon the basic faith-based principles they'd been reared with in their youth. When faced with a choice between the perceived excitement and good times they thought other people were having in the great and spacious building across the filthy river from the tree of life, they dropped the precious fruit they grew up with and headed down forbidden paths to try and cross the river to get to the party in the great and spacious building.

Along the way to the foundationless, floating building of "good" times, they suffered from what social psychologists call cognitive dissonance (CD). CD is an unsustainable and uncomfortable feeling caused by holding several contradictory ideas at the same time. The Savior explained it best: "No man can serve two masters: for either he will hate the one, and love the other; or else he will hold to the one, and despise the other. Ye cannot serve God and mammon" (Matthew 6:24).

We can't keep this up for long and will soon have to make a choice as to which master we'll serve. We either have to stop the behaviors and sins and repent or we have to change our attitudes and beliefs and choose to forget the correct principles that teach us the behavior is harmful. Many a wanderer has taken the easy path of discarding his or her faith instead of making the effort to break an addictive but no longer pleasurable behavior.

The problem with taking the easy road is explained in both the Old Testament and the Book of Mormon: "There is no peace, saith my God, to the wicked" (Isaiah 57:21). "Do not suppose, because it has been spoken concerning restoration, that ye shall be restored from sin to happiness. Behold, I say unto you, wickedness never was happiness" (Alma 41:10).

Many years ago, one woman told me she no longer believed in God. She then told me about an affair she'd had with her husband's boss. To relieve her guilt, she suggested to her husband that he might find some happiness in dating her best friend. Her husband agreed to this. In a short time, however, her husband's boss ended his relationship with her, and a week later her husband announced he was going to leave her and move in with her best friend. The woman was distraught and disillusioned with life, so she came for counseling. I know this sounds like a soap opera, but truth is often stranger than fiction when relationship principles are thrown out the window.

It doesn't matter if we say we no longer believe in the laws of nature and are going to ignore the law of gravity from now on. If we arrogantly step off a cliff, we'll suffer consequences as sure as the sun will rise tomorrow. We can say God's law of chastity or exclusivity in marriage doesn't apply to us, but in the end we don't really break God's laws upon which correct principles are based—we simply break ourselves against them. The woman found peace again only when she returned to the beliefs of her youth.

I learned an interesting lesson from the woman's husband when I met him. He fell passionately in "love" with his wife's best friend and, soon after moving in with her, said he wanted to divorce his wife and asked the friend to marry him. His wife's friend laughed and said, "Never!" She explained that she'd done that three times before: stolen someone else's husband, married them, and watched her new husband turn into a guilt-ridden, no-fun person who just laid around the house and mourned the damage he'd done to his first wife and children.

The husband also eventually woke up and went back to his wife. I helped them understand the benefits and blessings of the exclusivity principle, and they both vowed to live by it.

Chapter 1: Faith

The Pew Research Center revealed, in a 2013 publication entitled "The Decline of Institutional Religion," that fewer Americans identify with religion or practice it. The one group that is swelling in numbers is those with no religious affiliation. They are being referred to as *nones* in the press. In the 1950s, *nones* represented only about 2 percent of the population. In the 1970s, they were about 7 percent. Today, they are about 23 percent, but among eighteen to twenty-nine year olds, they are more than 30 percent.

The trend line for the decline in faith in God in America closely resembles the decline in marriage reported in the *Deseret News* on Febuary 19, 2015:

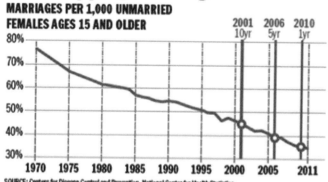

The dropping marriage rate

MARRIAGES PER 1,000 UNMARRIED FEMALES AGES 15 AND OLDER

SOURCE: Centers for Disease Control and Prevention, National Center for Health Statistics, and U.S. Census Bureau, Current Population Survey.

DESERET NEWS GRAPHIC

America, it appears, is headed in the opposite direction that the family proclamation counsels: "Successful marriages and families are established and maintained on principles of faith."

It's also fairly obvious that without faith, fewer people are forming committed relationships by marrying and bringing children into the world in a responsible manner. Not as many people have faith in God and choose to marry, start a family, or seriously think about what life will be like for them in eternity.

What is the world missing as a result of jumping overboard, abandoning faith, and choosing to swim alone in today's shark-infested waters? I personally think they're missing a lot.

Here is an example of how faith can help maintain a relationship formed by sacred covenants in the house of the Lord.

A close friend (an ear, noise, and throat surgeon) told of an interesting surgery he performed recently. A woman came to him with a tumor on her neck. He did a needle biopsy on it and sent it to the lab to see if it was cancerous. The report came back that it was benign and not life-threatening. He set a date to surgically remove the growth.

The growth was in an area of the neck that was close to a nerve that, if cut, would probably cause one side of her mouth to uncontrollably droop, so extra caution would need to be taken to not cut the nerve. As he started to perform the surgery, he was immediately presented with a serious problem. The nerve that controls the smile was directly over the tumor. Standard protocol said, in that situation and with that type of tumor, to cut around the nerve, leaving it undamaged, and take out as much of the growth as possible.

He started to do this but had a powerful feeling that he shouldn't follow protocol. He hesitated, thought it through again, and came to the same logical conclusion: don't cut the nerve. He started to carefully cut around the nerve and had an even more powerful feeling that this wasn't the right thing to do. He again hesitated and stopped. He went through the same steps a third time but again stopped.

By this time, the nurses were wondering what was going on and asked him if he was okay. He focused even harder and for the fourth time had the same strong impression that he should cut the nerve, completely remove the tumor, and cut away the area around it, leaving safe margins. He decided to follow his impressions and cut the nerve to be able to completely remove the tumor.

Afterward, he told the patient what he'd done and apologized for cutting the nerve, which had resulted in a slightly droopy smile on one side of her face, but it wasn't as bad as it could have been. He told her he had a strong impression that was the right thing to do. Surprisingly, she wasn't upset and told him that she was positive he had done the right thing because her bishop had given her a blessing and said that the Lord would guide the surgeon's hands.

Later, the tumor was sent to the lab to make sure it was what they thought it was. The lab frantically reported back to the doctor that they had made a terrible mistake in the first analysis and that the tumor was not only cancerous but was a rare, aggressive, and extremely fast-growing type of cancer that would've killed her in a matter of months had it not been fully removed in the manner he had done it.

There were several principles in play with this incident. First, the bishop needed the faith to give the correct blessing that could unlock the powers of heaven to help his ward member. Second, the woman needed to have the faith to be healed. Third, the surgeon needed to be in tune enough with the Spirit to hear and understand what the Lord was telling him to do. Fourth, the Lord needed to agree that the blessing given was the right thing to do for this woman at this time of her life. All these principles were correctly applied, and the miracle took place. Without faith, the woman would've died, and her husband and family would've had to carry on without her.

Principle Statement One

Successful marriages and families are established and maintained on the principle of faith.

Understanding Faith's Relationship to Love

In the most practical terms I can think of, the relationship between faith and true love is that we can't give the person we love something we don't have ourselves. If "God is love" (1 John 4:8) and we want to love others more perfectly, then we need to know and understand the God of love before we can love another perfectly. True love, eternal love of another human being cannot be given, understood, or received unless we first know God and receive the gift of love from Him.

In 1 John 4:8 and 16, the Apostle John said, "He that loveth not knoweth not God; for God is love. . . . And we have known and believed the love that God hath to us. God is love; and he that dwelleth in love dwelleth in God, and God in him." Just as developing faith in God is a process that takes time and effort, so does the development of love and faith in our partner. Again, keep in mind that Satan will do all he can to make sure this doesn't happen. Satan is real and wants nothing more than to knock you and your future or current spouse and family off the path leading to the celestial kingdom.

Elder Joseph B. Wirthlin of the Quorum of the Twelve Apostles warned us about Satan's power in the last days: "We live in a day when Lucifer's influence is greater than we ever have known in our lifetimes. In terms of the sin, evil, and wickedness upon the earth, we could liken our time to the days of Noah before the flood. No one is immune to affliction and difficulty, whether it be economical, emotional, or spiritual. Immorality, violence, and divorce, with their accompanying sorrows, plague society worldwide."[7]

To overcome Satan's opposition to our happiness, there are two separate paths we need to embark on that eventually merge into one strait and narrow road. The paths are the love of God and the love of an eternal mate. These are both similar and complementary to each other. Elder John A. Widtsoe taught, "True love of man for woman always includes love of God from whom all good things issue."[8] I believe we can modify this quote a little and it'll also be a true principle: True love for and faith in God always includes a love for His children—our fellow human beings.

Movement down either of these roads of faith automatically takes us down the other. The closer we become to God, the closer that new faith takes us to pure love for our partner. The greater our righteous and pure love for our partner becomes, the closer we become to God. I call this the "dual unity principle."

Dual Unity Principle

In Matthew 22:37 and 39, we have the classic description of dual unity—the first and great commandment for oneness with God is to "love the Lord thy God with all thy heart, and with all thy soul, and with all thy mind." The Savior then explained that the most practical application of the first great commandment (or path) is to work on the second pathway: "And the second is like unto it, Thou shalt love thy neighbour as thyself." It appears these two commandments are interrelated. To love God, learn to love His children. To be able to love His children, learn to love God.

I was coming home a few years ago from a trip to Washington, D.C., and was studying Alma 32 on the plane for a Book of Mormon institute class. I was also preparing a courtship lesson for a marriage class when I thought, *This is interesting*. Alma 32 is a well-known chapter that missionaries use to teach how to develop faith in God and the restored gospel. It details how our faith starts as a seed and grows to maturity. It then explains how to keep this fragile faith from failing.

It was interesting to see that Alma's fifteen steps to develop perfect faith in God are also the same steps that develop true love for another human being. Was it a coincidence? Would the Lord purposely do such a thing? Could this be an example of dualism? I believe sometimes God does things like this. Why wouldn't He? I sometimes give the same talk to two different audiences. Sometimes a single pattern or series of steps can be used to teach us how to arrive at different destinations.

Alma 32 is a lesson on faith in God and is also a lesson on how to find and develop pure love for an eternal companion, and I don't think it's an accident that they correlate so perfectly. Alma 32 is the practical application of Matthew 22 on how to achieve the first and great commandment to love God with all our heart, mind, and soul. Alma 32 also offers a step-by-step instruction manual on the second great commandment: to love our neighbors as ourselves. Maybe this is why the Savior, in referring to these two commandments, said, "On these two commandments hang all the law and the prophets" (Matthew 22:40).

Learning to obey these two commandmentsand apply them in a wide variety of circumstances appears to fulfill *all the law* and what we need to gain exaltation. We'll now examine Alma's chapter in detail and the fifteen steps. I think you will be surprised to see how appropriate the counsel is for both the development of faith and of true love that lasts for eternity.

Fifteen Applications of Faith in Finding and Keeping True Love

Alma's path to perfect faith in God and perfect love and unity with an eternal companion:

Application 1: Humility (Alma 32:5–13)

Verse 13 teaches the importance of humility in developing faith. "And now, because ye are compelled to be humble blessed are ye; for a man sometimes, if he is compelled to be humble, seeketh repentance; and now surely, whosoever repenteth shall find mercy; and he that findeth mercy and endureth to the end the same shall be saved."

Faith in God

Humility leads sincere truth-seekers to a readiness to believe and recognize the need for faith in God. They humbly place their own interests and passions second to doing the Lord's will. The Pharaoh of Egypt expressed the opposite of an attitude of faith in and dependence upon God: "And Pharaoh said, Who is the Lord, that I should obey his voice to let Israel go? I know not the Lord, neither will I let Israel go" (Exodus 5:2). This attitude was repeated by both King Noah, "Or who is the Lord, that shall bring upon my people such great affliction?" (Mosiah 11:27), and by Cain, "Who is the Lord that I should know him?" (Moses 5:16).

Love of an Eternal Mate

For singles, humility that leads to faith is a "not my way but thy way" attitude that leads to believing and acting upon the Lord's counsel that "it is not good that the man should be alone" (Genesis 2:18; Moses 3:18; Abraham 5:14). Humility in looking for an eternal mate leads us to ignore modern criticism of traditional covenant and commitment marriage. Today's growing distain for marriage is often based upon extreme individuality (selfishness), fear of failure (lack of faith), fear of sharing (materialism), fear of lifestyle change (hedonism), and plain shortsightedness. Humility leads the seeker of truth to trust in the plan of salvation (Alma 42:5), or the great plan of happiness (Alma 42:8), and to seek an eternal mate.

A lack of humility leads those not yet married (of both sexes) to look for an eternal mate only among those they consider physically attractive in the eyes of the world. One young student actually attended local beauty pageants for many years looking for the perfect wife. Apparently he failed to look in the mirror during those years, as he packed extra pounds on his body. It wasn't until he finally humbled himself in his late thirties and expanded and reprioritized his search criteria that he found his eternal companion.

In both courtship and marriage, there are many other ways humility prepares us for and maintains pure love. Humility causes us to look outward and recognize the needs of others, motivating us to sacrifice for them when necessary. If we aren't humble enough to sacrifice our self-interests and needs for the good of the relationship, then we're not ready for a marriage that will last.

Humility overcomes the stubborn pride that kills couple problem-solving skills and creates a willingness to compromise. Humility helps us not overestimate our own intelligence, talents, or beauty and attraction to others, thus expanding the field of potentially compatible eternal companions. These are but a few of the ways faith can bring us to humility and improve our chances of success in intimate relationships.

Application 2: Repentance (Alma 32:15)

"Yea, he that truly humbleth himself, and repenteth of his sins . . ."

Faith in God

Humility leads to godly sorrow, repentance, and receptiveness for the Holy Ghost to guide us in our pursuit of true faith in the Lord.

Love of an Eternal Mate

Before marriage, faith leads to the humility that motivates us to repent and become worthy to receive the guidance of the Holy Ghost that we so desperately need in seeking an eternal mate and learning to love him or her all our lives. In marriage, faith leads to the humility that motivates us to repent and be worthy of the guidance we need to be perceptive to our eternal mate's ever-changing needs. See chapter three for a more complete discussion of the importance of repentance in marriage.

Application 3: Patience, Long-Suffering (Alma 32:15)

This important character trait is expressed in the middle of verse 15: "and endureth to the end." Some modern relationship advice counsels the opposite of commitment and faithfully enduring to the end, such as "live for the moment" or, "take all you can get and get out." The Lord's counsel is different from the world's wisdom and is based upon patience and commitment to the end.

Faith in God

Acquiring true faith in God requires patience, long-suffering, and enduring to the end of our journey to achieve this worthy goal.

Love of an Eternal Mate

Before marriage, taking a relationship all the way to the altar often requires great patience, long-suffering, and endurance. There may be doubts and a breaking off from the courtship process prematurely only to discover—after a period of agony—that you can't let the other person go. This process, which can take weeks or months to play out, may seem like an eternity for those trying to do what's right.

Nearly every semester that I teach institute and BYU marriage classes, there are one or two students who panic after becoming engaged and think about backing out, despite many of them receiving strong spiritual confirmations that the relationship is right and being greatly attracted to their chosen mates. They think about backing out even though there are no new negative findings about their mates or any specific disapproving incident—they simply get scared. It's similar to the fear of conversion that every missionary has watched his or her investigators go through as they try to discover and act upon newly discovered truth.

Engaged or nearly engaged couples worries include such things as finances, adjustment to sexual intimacy, what their families and friends think or *might* think about the marriage, whether they're still in love or not, and on and on. Their fears end up paralyzing and frustrating them because they cannot move forward with faith.

Those who are patient and allow their faith to overcome their fears succeed. Those who allow their fears to destroy their faith fail. 2 Timothy 1:7 gives some great counsel for people in these situations: "For God hath not given us the spirit of fear; but of power, and of love, and of a sound mind."

If we find ourselves fearful and doubting after we know it's right and there is no new revelation or incident, know that the fear and anxiety aren't coming from God. God gives us the gifts of power, love, and a sound mind for making good decisions, but never fear—that comes from the other direction.

After marriage, the faith that leads to patience and long-suffering is even more important. If we lose patience and fail to endure things like midlife crises or normal aging processes in our partner's life, we will fail to reach our divine destiny. Finding an eternal companion and staying married both require great faith, mature patience, and long-suffering. One possible definition of commitment is a willingness to be unhappy for a while.

Application 4: Stubbornness of Heart and Stubborn Pride (Alma 32:16)

Stubbornness kills opportunities to discover truth. Verse 16 reads, "Therefore, blessed are they who humble themselves without being compelled to be humble; or rather, in other words, blessed is he that believeth in the word of God, and is baptized without stubbornness of heart, yea, without being brought to know the word, or even compelled to know, before they will believe."

Faith in God

In searching for truth about God, it's far better to discover faith without our Creator having to provide humbling circumstances that encourage us to repent and remember Him. Our love for the forbidden sometimes makes it difficult for us to forsake our sins and find true faith.

Love of an Eternal Mate

Before marriage, hardness of heart can kill any relationship. It can be something like "kicking against the pricks" and ignoring God's counsel that it is not good to be alone. It can be a refusal to give up the perceived excitement of being single. It can be a refusal to accept the responsibilities of marriage and parenthood, even if we know the right one has come along. Stubbornness of heart can result in being pulled into the dark world where everything of importance is pushed aside for other, lesser pleasures.

After marriage, refusal to repent of hardness of heart or stubborn pride often leads to divorce for a multitude of reasons. We are blessed when we voluntarily strive to follow the Lord's counsel to come unto Him rather than being forced to give up our great stubbornness of heart through humbling circumstances, either provided by the Lord or as natural consequences of our own behavior.

Application 5: Don't Expect Signs (Alma 32:17–18)

As these verses say: "Yea, there are many who do say: If thou wilt show unto us a sign from heaven, then we shall know of a surety; then we shall believe. Now I ask, is this faith? Behold, I say unto you, Nay; for if a man knoweth a thing he hath no cause to believe, for he knoweth it."

Faith in God

The great plan of salvation does not include finding faith in God through signs that require no personal responsibility to discover truth. Knowledge of God is reserved for those who put forth a great discovery effort, sometimes over long periods of time, and then patiently wait for God to confirm. After all: "For we know that it is by grace that we are saved, after all we can do" (2 Nephi 25:23).

Love of an Eternal Mate

Before marriage, many feel the responsibility to discover their own eternal companion is too great a task and are paralyzed by the fear of making a bad decision. They ask for a sign from God that will relieve them of accountability for their choices. I believe we are expected to use wise agency and inspiration in finding true love, just as we are in finding true faith in God.

The choice of an eternal mate is one of both agency and inspiration. Elder Bruce R. McConkie told BYU students in 1975 the same thing in a talk entitled "Agency or Inspiration?" (*New Era*, January 1975, 38–43). We are expected to use our best decision-making skills and take our conclusion to the Lord for confirmation.

After marriage, we still have to make sound, life-changing decisions. Some of the most difficult decisions include such things as when to start a family, whether the wife should work outside the home (see chapter ten), how many children to have, whether to adopt or not, career choices, and so forth. We are expected to do our research, fast and pray, and ask for guidance—but not for a sign.

Application 6: You Have to Believe It's Possible (Alma 32:22)

Verse 22 of Alma 32 reads, "And now, behold, I say unto you, and I would that ye should remember, that God is merciful unto all who believe on his name; therefore he desireth, in the first place, that ye should believe, yea, even on his word."

Faith in God

God desires for us to believe in Him and will help us develop our faith. We need to first have the simple, optimistic faith to believe that it is possible to know God and discover that He loves us and truly desires to care for us.

Love of an Eternal Mate

God wants us to find an eternal mate. That truth is taught early in the Bible, in Genesis 2:18: "It is not good that the man should be alone." We need the faith to desire to complete this part of God's plan for us and to believe in our own abilities to accomplish the task. I've counseled with literally hundreds of young adults over the years who lost hope for a while that they would ever find an eternal companion. The vast majority of them have successfully done so.

If married and struggling in your marriage, the first step to recovery is to believe that the damage can be repaired and your marriage made whole again. The faintest optimistic belief can lead to a powerful faith that is capable of healing damaged relationships in time if we are just willing to try, try, and try again. We must first be willing to believe that it can be saved and commit to the healing process.

Application 7: There's a Help Desk (Alma 32:23)

"And now, he imparteth his word by angels unto men, yea, not only men but women also. Now this is not all; little children do have words given unto them many times, which confound the wise and the learned."

Faith in God

It's common practice for God to give inspiration to men, women, and even children to help us discover truth and developing faith. We must first research what has already been said by God in the scriptures about our questions, ponder our findings, and then call the help desk (mighty prayer) and ask for either confirmation of our decisions or help with the answers.

Love of an Eternal Mate

If unmarried, likewise it is possible for God to help us find an eternal mate, to confirm that our decision is right, and to bestow upon us the gift and ability to truly love another. All we have to do is ask in faith and listen for an answer, even if it takes more time than we'd like.

Married or single, it is our absolute right to pray to our Father in heaven and ask Him for help with our intimate relationships. We need to have faith and believe that happiness is possible. God will answer our sincere petitions.

Application 8: Faith and Love Take Time (Alma 32:26–27)

There's a process to developing faith and love: "Now, as I said concerning faith—that it was not a perfect knowledge—even so it is with my words. Ye cannot know of their surety at first, unto perfection, any more than faith is a perfect knowledge. But behold, if ye will awake and arouse your faculties, even to an experiment upon my words, and exercise a particle of faith, yea, even if ye can no more than desire to believe, let this desire work in you, even until ye believe in a manner that ye can give place for a portion of my words."

Faith in God

Obtaining perfect faith in God is a process that often takes time to develop. The process begins by awakening and arousing our faculties to be willing to experiment on the words of Christ. We must be willing to desire to believe. Our attitude is everything. We must be optimistic and believe that perfect faith in God is achievable.

Love of an Eternal Mate

When unmarried, knowing if a relationship is right is a process that also takes time. It begins with an awakening and arousal of our faculties (mental powers or abilities). We must be willing to apply ourselves to the task with all diligence. To experiment means we are willing to engage in the dating game optimistically. We must be willing to get back into the game even after difficult defeats or setbacks.

I remember one enthusiastic recently returned missionary taking a marriage class from me. He told me his goal was to be engaged by the end of the semester. Every week during the semester, he reported his progress on the girls he had met and dated. The semester ended and he was a bit frustrated. He continued to tell me about his dates each week for the rest of the school year until one day he told me that he had dated over fifty girls that year and felt that he "had looked under every rock."

He remained upbeat and kept his desire high to find an eternal mate compatible with his interests and goals. Finally, one-and-a-half years after setting his original goal, he brought his fiancée in to meet me. She was perfect for him and well worth the effort and wait.

It doesn't have to take that long. I met my wife-to-be the first day of college. She was from Texas and I was from Oregon. We met at the University of Utah. It was almost like she had a neon sign over her head that read, "Here she is." We went on our first date that night and were married three years later. It started fast and I soon believed it was right but later learned the truth of "ye cannot know of their surety at first, unto perfection." Over time and after a couple of near breakups and my going on a mission, we both figured it out and came to the point of "let this desire work in you, even until ye believe in a manner that ye can give place for a portion of my words."

For those already married, sometimes the marriage can get in so much trouble that this entire process needs to be repeated. The road to recovery includes an awakening and arousal of our faculties and a willingness to experiment and try to pull things together again. We need to "exercise a particle of faith" and agree to begin the healing process. It's harder the second or third time around because so much water has passed under the bridge. The formula for fixing a marriage however is perfectly laid out before us in Alma's words. All we need to do is to "let this desire work in you" and stay committed and dedicated to the task.

Application 9: Doubt and Fear Kill Growth (Alma 32:28–29)

"Now, we will compare the word unto a seed. Now, if ye give place, that a seed may be planted in your heart, behold, if it be a true seed, or a good seed, if ye do not cast it out by your unbelief, that ye will resist the Spirit of the Lord, behold, it will begin to swell within your breasts; and when you feel these swelling motions, ye will begin to say within yourselves—It must needs be that this is a good seed, or that the word is good, for it beginneth to enlarge my soul; yea, it beginneth to enlighten my understanding, yea, it beginneth to be delicious to me. Now behold, would not this increase your faith? I say unto you, Yea; nevertheless it hath not grown up to a perfect knowledge."

Faith in God

Perfect faith is compared to a seed. If we are willing to experiment and plant a seed—if we don't cast it out with unbelief where we resist the Spirit of God bearing truth unto us—then faith begins to grow as our efforts and the power of the Spirit work together to enlighten our understanding. However, even though our faith has increased, it is not yet perfect.

Love of an Eternal Mate

For those unmarried, perfect love is compared to a seed. If you're willing to experiment and plant a seed (go on a date and go again)—if you do not cast it out before you know enough about your date and don't ignore the Spirit—then you can begin to feel that this might be someone special. These feelings of rapport and comfort grow into feelings of care, responsibility, respect, and knowledge (see chapter six) for and of your new companion. Your love is still not perfect or complete but it's on its way, though it may be too soon to make a judgment.

If married, renewing love in a marriage can work in the same way. There must be a desire to replant the seed and a willingness to experiment one more time. Alma also says that the seed must be a "true seed" if it's going to work. Frankly, some relationships *should* end before marriage. Sometimes even temple-sealed eternal relationships should also end under certain conditions. For more information on this, please see the quotation by President Faust in chapter four (page 59).

Application 10: The Similarity Principle (Alma 32:31)

"And now, behold, are ye sure that this is a good seed? I say unto you, Yea; for every seed bringeth forth unto its own likeness."

Faith in God

Because of the growth of the seed, we logically conclude it's a good seed because "every seed bringth forth unto its own likeness." We learned these truths before coming to this earth and believed them in our premortal existence. Now we relearn that which we knew before and it has a familiar "likeness." We find we enjoy associating and fellowshipping with like-minded people who have discovered the same truths and come to the same conclusions we have.

Love of an Eternal Mate

In most cases, "soul mates" are fictitious and an illusion. However, successful courtships discover many similarities with their chosen companion in beliefs, values, interests, personality traits, and the importance of the gospel in their lives. These likenesses draw them closer and increase feelings of trust, admiration, and love. One of the most solid, research-based principles in the social sciences is the similarity principle: "The more alike two people are in intimate relationships, (such as dating, courtship, and marriage), the greater the probability that the relationship will succeed."[9]

Once married, neither spouse should allow outside pursuits or hobbies to drive a wedge between them. It's not necessary or even desirable to do all things together or to have all the same interests. However, many marriages have been broken when a newfound hobby or interest becomes more important. There needs to remain through the lifetime of the marriage a set of core values and shared interests for the couple to work on together. More will be said on this when we discuss the ninth and last foundation stone, "wholesome recreational activities."

Application 11: Not Everything Is True (Alma 32:32)

The scripture for this application reads, "Therefore, if a seed groweth it is good, but if it groweth not, behold it is not good, therefore it is cast away."

Faith in God

There are many bogus belief systems advocated by false prophets and teachers today. One means of discerning validity is if the ideas persist and your belief in them increases over time. This idea is presented in Doctrine and Covenants 9:8: "But, behold, I say unto you, that you must study it out in your mind; then you must ask me if it be right, and if it is right I will cause that your bosom shall burn within you; therefore, you shall feel that it is right."

If there is no growth, Alma says to cast it away. This same idea is presented in Doctrine and Covenants 9:9, which says, "But if it be not right you shall have no such feelings, but you shall have a stupor of thought that shall cause you to forget the thing which is wrong." It is every person's responsibility to carefully and prayerfully determine fact from fiction. In speaking of the last days, in Mathew 24:4 states, "And Jesus answered and said unto them, Take heed that no man deceive you." Learning to determine truth from deception is one of the important tests of our mortal existence. "Prove all things; hold fast that which is good" (1 Thessalonians 5:21).

Love of an Eternal Mate

If dating and there is no growth in the feelings of love and trust, it may be because the relationship is not right for you and "therefore it is cast away." A lack of common values, goals, personality types, and poor dating experiences together can create these feelings.

If a breakup before marriage is necessary, it should be done gently, discreetly, and with prudence and great care for the feelings of another. I recall the shocked look on the face of one of my students in class one day when he glanced at his cell phone. I asked what was wrong. He exclaimed that he had just been told through a text message by his girlfriend and soon-to-be–fiancée that they were through. He said, "I can't believe she would do that through a text message!" Our electronic age seems to have diminished face-to-face communication skills.

After marriage, "casting away" a bad relationship is a serious decision. Again, I believe President Faust's counsel is the best there is. When people ask me if I think their situation is bad enough to qualify as an irredeemable relationship that is destructive of a person's dignity as a human being, I ask them where they were married. If the answer is in the temple, then I suggest they go back to the temple as often as it takes until they get their answer.

Application 12: Our Faith Is Dormant (Alma 32:33–34)

"And now, behold, because ye have tried the experiment, and planted the seed, and it swelleth and sprouteth, and beginneth to grow, ye must needs know that the seed is good. And now, behold, is your knowledge perfect? Yea, your knowledge is perfect in that thing, and your faith is dormant; and this because you know, for ye know that the word hath swelled your souls, and ye also know that it hath sprouted up, that your understanding doth begin to be enlightened, and your mind doth begin to expand."

Faith in God

The growing seed leads us to believe it is good. However, is our belief in the seed a perfect knowledge yet? Yes and no. We can know perfectly that it's true, but that does not mean we have a perfect understanding of all its nature yet. The gospel is vast and there is much to learn, and our "faith is dormant." It takes time for faith to mature and be replaced with a perfect knowledge. Few accomplish this in their lifetime.

Love of an Eternal Mate

To the nearly engaged, it is the same with a newfound eternal mate. We can know they are true and compatible for us and our knowledge of this may be perfect. However, like perfect faith, true love lays dormant until it has time to mature by thousands of experiences. Also, for it to be true love, it has to be reciprocal, meaning two-way love.

If a potential eternal companion-to-be is at a different point in the selection process, it requires discipline and patience waiting for them to catch up. Love often has differing maturation rates at the beginning and throughout the history of the relationship.

I recall a young woman in a marriage prep class who confided to the class that she was in a state of total confusion about whom to marry as she had two offers at the same time. She had promised to wait for a missionary who still had four months to go on his mission. She'd corresponded weekly with the missionary for twenty months and he'd indicated he was still quite interested in marrying her. In the meantime, she was dating a returned missionary who had arrived at application fifteen in the development of true love. He knew she was the one for him, and his knowledge of this mystery was perfect in his mind and his faith that she was perfect for him was complete, so he had asked her to marry him.

The young woman was honest with both young men and told each about the other. I know this is beginning to sound like an episode of *The Bachelorette*. Both said they would be patient and wait for her to decide. For the next four months, she went back and forth and shared her conflicted feelings with our class each week. Finally, two weeks before the missionary was to return home, she told the returned missionary they were not to see each other again for a month so she could give her soon-to-return missionary a fair chance.

Here is where step one is important. How many male readers would be humble enough to patiently wait for a month, being shut out of any chance to compete? This returned missionary waited patiently until the young lady called him three and a half weeks later to say she wanted him back and if he would still have her, she would marry him. This young man was that humble and that patient. They are now in the process of living happily ever after . . . for eternity.

For those married, when does married love become a perfect love with complete understanding and knowledge of one other? This question reminds me of a novelty book I saw once. The cover title was *Everything Man Has Learned about Women from Adam Forward.* When I opened it and thumbed through, I saw that every page was blank. The book idea was humorous and points out how hard it can be to know everything about one other, but that's not entirely true. With commitment, patience, and effort, we can learn a great deal about our eternal mate. It is a lifelong process, however, as both spouses age and learn and try to adapt to ever-evolving circumstances. The target of true, eternal love is a moving target that requires constant attention and fine adjustments to hit consistently. How love evolves is discussed in chapters six and seven.

Application 13: Falling in Love Is Just the Beginning (Alma 32:35–36)

"O then, is not this real? I say unto you, Yea, because it is light; and whatsoever is light, is good, because it is discernible, therefore ye must know that it is good; and now behold, after ye have tasted this light is your knowledge perfect? Behold I say unto you, Nay; neither must ye lay aside your faith, for ye have only exercised your faith to plant the seed that ye might try the experiment to know if the seed was good."

Faith in God

Because light is discernable, we can know the object of our faith is good and true. However, we need to remember that the discovery of new faith is not an end in itself. Finding faith in something that is true is just the beginning of a long and often arduous journey, fraught with perils and many kinds of tests before that faith is mature and fruitful. We know it is true, and this is real and wonderful. However, compared to all there is to know about God, we should realize we don't know all that much and should strive to learn all we can in the years to come.

Love of an Eternal Mate

For singles and married couples alike, love—like light—is also discernable and we can usually know fairly soon if the object of our love is good for us or not. Like faith, that takes time and testing by experiences to become perfect knowledge and true, mature, full-blown, eternal love. It requires the same patience, time, and sacrifices. Falling in love and getting married is the *beginning* of the incredible journey, not the end. We know we are in love and that is wonderful, but again, compared to all there is to learn about true and pure love, we should realize that we are but novices.

Application 14: Seeds and Fruit (Alma 32:37, Deuteronomy 24:5)

"And behold, as the tree beginneth to grow, ye will say: Let us nourish it with great care, that it may get root, that it may grow up, and bring forth fruit unto us. And now behold, if ye nourish it with much care it will get root, and grow up, and bring forth fruit."

Faith in God

A new testimony is a precious and fragile thing that must be nourished with great care. The seed must be allowed to take root deep in fertile soil to grow into a tree that can produce desirable fruit. A new testimony of God must be fed on a daily basis. Prayer, scripture reading, association with others of like faith, and fulfilling callings are all ways to nourish the seed.

Love of an Eternal Mate

Newlyweds, consider Deuteronomy 24:5, which reads, "When a man hath taken a new wife, he shall not go out to war, neither shall he be charged with any business: but he shall be free at home one year, and shall cheer up his wife which he hath taken."

In the Old Testament, a newlywed man was exempt from war for one year so he and his new wife could adjust to each other. It wasn't a bad idea. Compared to what true love can become, young love is also like a tiny seed that must be nurtured and cared for over a long time before it can produce the fulness of the precious fruit that it's potentially capable of.

Many of the Church's leaders have advocated the importance of continued courtship after the marriage ceremony. This may be one of the most repeated counsels that the Brethren have given over the years. We will discuss this topic more in the chapter on wholesome recreational activities.

Application 15: The Tree of Life (Alma 32:40–43)

"And thus, if ye will not nourish the word, looking forward with an eye of faith to the fruit thereof, ye can never pluck of the fruit of the tree of life. But if ye will nourish the word, yea, nourish the tree as it beginneth to grow, by your faith with great diligence, and with patience, looking forward to the fruit thereof, it shall take root; and behold it shall be a tree springing up unto everlasting life. And because of your diligence and your faith and your patience with the word in nourishing it, that it may take root in you, behold, by and by ye shall pluck the fruit thereof, which is most precious, which is sweet above all that is sweet, and which is white above all that is white, yea, and pure above all that is pure; and ye shall feast upon this fruit even until ye are filled, that ye hunger not, neither shall ye thirst. Then, my brethren, ye shall reap the rewards of your faith, and your diligence, and patience, and long-suffering, waiting for the tree to bring forth fruit unto you."

Faith in God

The fruit of mature faith grows on the tree of life. The fruit is possible exaltation and a fulness of joy that is only found completely in eternal marriage and the eternal lives that result from that sacred union. It comes only to those who care about, take great thought for, and continue to nourish the tree all the days of their lives.

Love of an Eternal Mate

The fruit of mature love also grows on the tree of life. That fruit consists of perfect unity, resulting in being conjointly elected into the Church of the firstborn, enjoying a fulness of joy in the continuation of the marriage forever, and sitting down with our Savior as joint-heirs in His kingdom and glory.

It's only in the new and everlasting covenant of marriage that we are able to use our divine nature to achieve our divine destiny. It's interesting that Alma ends the chapter at the tree of life. We achieve our divine destiny by partaking of the fruit of the tree of life. Could the fruit represent achieving exaltation by becoming like God, being eternally married with the ability to create eternal progeny? The dream's symbolism probably has multiple meanings and interpretations. I think one interpretation is that it's all about eternal marriage and Satan's opposition to this great plan of happiness. I can easily visualize those standing in the large and spacious building pointing at and mocking those who have partaken of the fruit of the tree and chosen to defy the wisdom of their world and marry in the temple of the Lord.

Those in the building who are angry with and critical of the Lord's true plan for men and women have to take forbidden paths and then cross the filthy river and "great and terrible gulf" that separates them from the tree of life. In their search for worldly stimulation and satisfaction, they fail to understand there is no success on earth that compensates for a failure to form an eternal marriage and family. All other successes are like a foundationless building, floating in the air, waiting for a small wind to come along and blow it over.

Lehi's vision is exacting in its simplicity and clear in the consequences of being seduced into these forbidden paths. The only true and lasting happiness in this life is found in the fruit of the tree of life: an eternal marriage based upon true love and the children born of that love. This fact has got to drive Satan mad with jealousy and envy because he wants nothing more than to make you and me as miserable as he is.

Summary

The price for a strong testimony of the true and living God and perfect love and unity with an eternal mate are the same as the merchant's payment to find the flawless pearl: "Who, when he had found one *pearl of great price*, went and sold all that he had, and bought it" (Matthew 13:46, emphasis added). This chapter has reviewed some of the payment required for such purchases, as taught by Alma. Areas that improve the faith needed to establish and maintain a marriage include such foundational rocks as humility, repentance, patience, a lack of pride, willingness to make decisions by and for yourself with the Lord's confirmation, and obedience to the teachings of the plan of salvation.

In finding and keeping an eternal mate, it helps not to judge too quickly (nor give up too soon), to pray for help, to control our doubts and fears, and to be cautious in accepting the counsel of friends and relatives. When a relationship shows promise, don't panic and withdraw, taking counsel from your fears. After marriage, record and always remember the good times.

But before marriage, know that not all relationships are meant to be and have the courage to cast out a bad seed and start again if there is too much dissimilarity in things that are of eternal importance. Some relationships can be harmful to our emotional and physical well-being. Fasting, prayer, temple attendance, and obedience to the promptings of the Spirit can help us make wise decisions in these sensitive situations.

Not all relationships develop at the same pace. Patience is often required in waiting for a potential eternal mate to catch up and become equally yoked. Getting married isn't the end. Continued courtship, attention to detail, and daily safeguarding is required to maintain an eternal relationship. Enduring to the end in happiness requires a tremendous commitment and requires that we place marriage at the highest level of our priorities.

What follows is a self-evaluation quiz. There may be other areas where your relationship skills need to be strengthened. Please evaluate each question and ask yourself what you can do to improve in these areas, and then come up with a plan to do so.

The Principle of Faith Self-Evaluation Questions

Application 1: Humility. Are the will of the Lord and the plan of salvation more important to me than the wisdom of world and its criticism and disdain for traditional and committed marriage? For married couples: As my eternal mate and I change physically over the years, will I still see us as we once were and will be again?

Application 2: Repentance. For singles and married couples: Has your faith led to repentance that qualifies you for the daily guidance of the Holy Ghost in your relationships?

Application 3: Patience, long-suffering. For singles and married couples: Are you patient enough to wait for a relationship to grow and reach maturity?

Application 4: Stubbornness of heart. Is there anything in your life that detracts from your ability to be led by the Spirit that you are just not ready and willing to give up? What effect is this stubbornness having on your relationships?

Application 5: Don't ask for a sign. Can you make an important decision on your own and take your answer to the Lord to receive a confirmation or stupor of thought?

Application 6: Belief. If single, do you believe that it's possible to find an eternal mate? If married, do you believe your marriage can improve?

Application 7: There's a help desk. How would you rate your ability to ask God in faith when you need help?

Application 8: Faith and love take time. If single, can you get back into the dating game after a disappointing failure? Are you committed to keep trying?

Application 9: Doubt and fear kill growth. If single, have you ever cast away a potentially good relationship match because you "cast it out by your unbelief, that ye will resist the Spirit of the Lord"? If married, when disagreements cause hurt and anger, do you strive to quickly and maturely resolve the issue or do you feed the anger and pride until you make a mountain out of a molehill? Have you ever allowed your anger to "cast it out (*it* is all the good things about your marriage or relationship) by your unbelief" (unbelief is a lack of perspective brought about by a lack of faith)? Can you control your negative thoughts about your partner, eliminate them, and replace them with thoughts about all the good there is in your partner and your relationship?

Application 10: The similarity principle. If single, what area of similarity is most important to you in a potential mate? Which ones are deal breakers? If married, what efforts have you made or are you willing to make to ensure that you and your mate do not draw too far apart in your interests and activities as the years pass by?

Application 11: Not everything is true. If single, have you allowed for the possibility that the relationship might not be right? Are the Spirit and your mind leading the way in the decision-making process?

Application 12: Our faith is dormant. If single, are you willing to be patient and wait for a potential mate who has not yet come to the same conclusion that you have about the relationship being right? If married, can you patiently wait for a mate to catch up with you if you have become unequally yoked? How committed are you to keeping the relationship alive?

Application 13: Falling in love is just the beginning. If married, are you sufficiently aware that perfect, true love will take a lifetime to develop? Are you patient enough to give yourself and your eternal companion the room and the time to grow into it?

Application 14: Seeds and fruit. For newlyweds: Are you working hard to not allow any obligations to crowd out time for courtship? Is your partner still your number one priority?

Application 15: The tree of life. For both those engaged and married: How much diligence, faith, and patience are you willing to put forth into establishing and maintaining a successful marriage and family? Where is this goal on your life's priorities list? How committed are you to achieving it?

Chapter 2: Prayer

S uccessful marriages and families are established and maintained on the principle of prayer.

Understanding the Prayer Principle

The purpose of prayer is not to try to change the will of God, but rather to obtain blessings that God is already willing to grant, either for us or for others. The blessings are awaiting us. They are part of our divine nature, but God requires we take the initiative to ask.[10]

Though there are many things that can be said about prayer, here are four general principles:

1. We should pray to the Father in Christ's name. "And whatsoever ye shall ask in my name, that will I do, that the Father may be glorified in the Son. If ye shall ask any thing in my name, I will do it" (John 14:13–14). "And in that day ye shall ask me nothing. Verily, verily, I say unto you, Whatsoever ye shall ask the Father in my name, he will give it you" (John 16:23).

2. Our intents and desires need to be the same as Christ's intents and desires for us. "If ye abide in me, and my words abide in you, ye shall ask what ye will, and it shall be done unto you" (John 15:7). "He that asketh in the Spirit asketh according to the will of God; wherefore it is done even as he asketh" (D&C 46:30).

3. We should be careful to ask for things that are right in God's eyes, thus making it possible for God to grant our petitions. "And whatsoever ye shall ask the Father in my name, which is right, believing that ye shall receive, behold it shall be given unto you" (3 Nephi 18:20).

4. We should refrain from prayers that originate in selfish or self-serving, unrighteous desires. "Ye ask, and receive not, because ye ask amiss, that ye may consume it upon your lusts" (James 4:3). "For verily I say unto you, they are given for the benefit of those who love me and keep all my commandments, and him that seeketh so to do; that all may be benefited that seek or that ask of me, that ask and not for a sign that they may consume it upon their lusts" (D&C 46:9). Inappropriate and selfish prayers can even turn to our condemnation: "And if ye ask anything that is not expedient for you, it shall turn unto your condemnation" (D&C 88:65).

Practical Applications of the Prayer Principle in Finding and Keeping True Love

There are many ways prayer can help establish and maintain eternal relationships. A few of these include finding the right one, being saved by grace, developing your relationship with Him who is "mighty to save," praying for your own well-being and development, praying for the needs of your loved ones, praying for the guidance of the Holy Ghost, effective prayer making us better listeners, seeing the results of powerful prayer, and praying for a positive attitude.

Application 1: Finding the Right One

If single, faithful prayer can help us keep an optimistic attitude about the possibility of finding an eternal mate and family—and when we do find someone, it can help us with the final decision.

No one should enter into marriage after finding a potential mate without having that decision confirmed to him or her through faithful prayer. As we discussed in the previous chapter, God is not likely to send an angel to personally make the choice for you. Additionally, there are no guarantees that your partner will not someday use their agency to make really dumb decisions that will be painful to you. There is, however, an absolute guarantee that God will always be there for you, listening to your pleas and counseling you at every step of this important journey. All you need to do is qualify and learn how to ask and listen for His answers.

One young woman shared this experience about prayer:

> My husband and I started praying together while we were still in the dating portion of our relationship and in the process of deciding if marriage was the right thing to do. After we started talking about it, Satan let loose his dogs and we were attacked with fears, doubts, struggles, and stresses that did not exist before. We decided to combat these attacks with prayer. After we joined forces and prayed together, we were better able to face those hardships. When praying together one night, my husband told me that he received his answer and knew that he wanted to marry me (unfortunately, it took a little bit more persuading on my part). We were swamped with stresses from school and we decided to go on a night hike. We reached the top of one of my husband's favorite mountain and we kneeled in prayer and asked/ begged our Heavenly Father to let us know if we were supposed to get married. While I didn't get a direct answer, it was so refreshing to know that I trusted this man enough to pray with him.
>
> Not only did praying together enhance our dating relationship then, it is a force that glues our marriage together now. We take turns praying every night together. It has become such an important part of our day that I cannot go to sleep without this ritual. Through these prayers, I've gotten to know my husband more, we've united, and we've both come closer to God.

Application 2: Saved by Grace

Another relationship of prayer to true love is "for we know that it is by grace that we are saved, after all we can do" (2 Nephi 25:23). Continuing with the Alma 32 analogy of the seed from the last chapter, Alma tells us how to plant a seed. There are many things we need to do to have a successful harvest. We plant the seed, cultivate it, nourish it, and weed the seedbeds to give the seed a chance to sprout and grow. In the end, however, only God can cause the miracle that makes a seed sprout and grow to maturity. We can do a lot to provide a positive environment for the miracle of eternal love to happen, but in the end, we have to step back and ask the Lord to do what we can't do for ourselves.

If single, we do all that we can to provide the environment for love and marriage to take root and grow. Elder Joe J. Christenson, speaking to young adults about looking their best, commented, "Occasionally, look in a full-length mirror. Certainly we should not become obsessed with how we look but we should work to improve our physical appearance."[11]

If married and looking for ways to influence your partner's behavior, you should consider praying for him or her instead of using some of the more common and traditional ways marriage partners have used. Praying for your partner instead of using natural man control techniques like nagging, threatening, passive aggressive persuasions, pleading, hysterical crying, and angry shouting can produce miracles. There is much we can do to influence one another, but we certainly need to face the fact that changing others is out of our control.

Though God has the power to "soften hearts"—as He did with Nephi so that Nephi would believe the words of his father (1 Nephi 2:16) or with Ishmael and his household so they would go into the wilderness with Lehi (1 Nephi 7:5)—I'm not aware of any incident where God caused a person to fall in love in answer to someone else's prayers.

I believe that in order to receive the true love of a potential eternal mate, it's up to us and requires our best courting behavior. We can pray not to say or do anything stupid and we can pray for the opportunity to meet someone suitable, but the decision to be loved by another person is an essential part of his or her agency, and I believe God will always respect that agency.

Application 3: Developing Your Relationship with Him Who Is "Mighty to Save"

The Lord counsels the farmer in Alma 34:24 to "cry unto him over the crops of your fields, that ye may prosper in them." The maker of heaven and earth expects us to acknowledge the precarious and random nature of life and to stay in touch and ask for help as we try to provide shelter and produce our daily bread.

Alma's counsel is similar for intimate relationships. In Alma 34:17, we are taught to "begin to exercise your faith unto repentance, that ye begin to call upon his holy name, that he would have mercy upon you." Effective prayer, like faith, takes time to develop and begins with conforming our will and behavior to the Lord's. By doing so, we "begin to exercise [our] faith unto repentance," and then we can "begin to call upon his holy name" and the process of receiving mercy from the Lord through answered prayers is begun. Alma reminds us in verse 18 of the great power that God has to help and that He is "mighty to save."

Whether it's a prayer to be at your best and to have the opportunity to meet someone when single or for a married couple that desperately needs inspiration to say and do the right things, God is "mighty to save" and wants to hear from us.

Application 4: Praying for Your Own Well-Being and Development

In Alma 34:19, we are told, "Yea, humble yourselves and continue in prayer unto him." In verse 20, we learn to pray over our livelihood and attempts to provide: "Cry unto him when ye are in your fields, yea over all your flocks." We can't love and help others effectively if we're weighed down with problems.

In finding an eternal mate, we need to pray to have something to offer when the right one comes along. We can pray for help in our schooling, training, and work. Husbands should pray for the ability to provide, protect, preside, and help their wives to nurture. Wives can pray for the ability to nurture or whatever else is necessary for them to keep their family together and succeed. When our own lives are in order, then we can move to the next step of prayer, which is to pray for our immediate loved ones.

Application 5: Praying for the Needs of Your Loved Ones

Alma 34:21 counsels us to pray "in our houses, yea over all your household, both morning, mid-day, and evening." To me, this implies a real commitment to know the needs of my family and to be anxiously concerned about their welfare. The vast majority of mothers do this naturally for their children. They know their children's hurts and delights, their friends and schedules, and even what goes on behind closed doors. They set a high standard for concern and knowledge. Married couples should have that same level of genuine, consistent concern and researched knowledge about each other if they ever hope to reach the Lord's standard for eternal love and perfect unity.

How powerful can effective prayer for others be? Jesus Christ set the example for us: "And no tongue can speak, neither can there be written by any man, neither can the hearts of men conceive so great and marvelous things as we both saw and heard Jesus speak; and no one can conceive of the joy which filled our souls at the time we heard him pray for us unto the Father" (3 Nephi 17:17).

What if we could pray like this for our loved ones? What if we could pray for them like this in their hour of need—when they aren't making good decisions, when their behavior makes them so unlovable and obnoxious that we don't even want to be around them? What if we prayed powerfully for them instead of reverting to behaviors that come so naturally, such as nagging, criticizing, and condemning? Here are a few scriptures that encourage us to pray for our wayward loved ones instead of condemning them:

- "But ye shall pray for them, and shall not cast them out; and if it so be that they come unto you oft ye shall pray for them unto the Father, in my name" (3 Nephi 18:23).
- "Nevertheless, ye shall not cast him out from among you, but ye shall minister unto him and shall pray for him unto the Father, in my name; and if it so be that he repenteth and is baptized in my name, then shall ye receive him, and shall minister unto him of my flesh and blood" (3 Nephi 18:30).
- "But behold I say unto you, love your enemies, bless them that curse you, do good to them that hate you, and pray for them who despitefully use you and persecute you" (3 Nephi 12:44).

So you might ask, "Do these scriptures really apply to marriage?" Unfortunately, few couples go the distance without, in a moment of confusion or anger, temporarily viewing each other as the enemy and thinking about hating them just a little, or are tempted to spitefully use and persecute them. The scripture probably has its best application in long-term marriage.

Those of you who are single and reading this might think, *Yikes, why would I want to get into something like that?* The answer lies in reaching your divine destiny and deciding if it's worth the effort. It is, and in the process over time, if we develop self-control and are led by the Spirit, we will grow and develop patience that can be obtained in no other way. We become new creatures, born again to a higher level of existence with a more refined and godlike temperament and character. An eternity of happiness and joy is worth the struggle.

Application 6: Praying for the Guidance of the Holy Ghost

As we follow the counsel to pray for each other, what should we pray for when a loved one has gone a little wacky (at least from our perspective)? That answer is also found in 3 Nephi: "And they did pray for that which they most desired; and they desired that the Holy Ghost should be given unto them" (3 Nephi 19:9).

How many times have we tried to correct undesirable behavior in others and our communications with them have only made things worse? There are a few general communication principles we can employ that will increase our chances of success, but the most important communication technique of all is to be led by the Spirit to say and do the right things. The Spirit might even tell us to keep our mouths shut, forgive them, forget it, and just be nice.

Or on other occasions, we may be inspired to be proactive and lay it all out: "Reproving betimes with sharpness, when moved upon by the Holy Ghost; and then showing forth afterwards an increase of love toward him whom thou hast reproved, lest he esteem thee to be his enemy" (D&C 121:43). One of the secrets to an eternal marriage is to not turn those we love into our most intimate enemy.

Application 7: Effective Prayer Making Us Better Listeners

Powerful prayer entails more than talking to God and asking for things we think we need. Years ago during my doctoral studies at BYU, I was asked to pick up a distinguished visiting professor from the airport. He and his wife were recognized as pioneers in the field of family studies. They were scheduled to give two days of lectures and seminars at BYU. During those two days, every class and seminar they attended was started with prayer, and I noticed they listened intently and asked questions about the Latter-day Saints and our beliefs and practices.

As I drove them back to the airport, I asked them what they thought about their experience with the Mormons and their visit to BYU. The husband responded that he and his wife were Quakers and gave this observation: He said Mormons give many prayers and talk to God a lot. Quakers, however, spend more time listening to what God has to say to them than most Mormons seem to do. I had to agree that he might have a point.

How effective can prayer be when we also listen to what God wants of us? Could this developed skill also help us listen to our eternal mate more intently and better discover their desires of us? Could this skill lead to greater love for one another? I definitely think so.

Application 8: Seeing the Results of Powerful Prayer

Then at the other end of the spectrum is Alma's great-great-great grandson, Nephi. This powerful prophet demonstrated effective prayer and the resulting perfect unity with God. He also showed us what our potential divine nature is and what it can do for us in finding or improving eternal love.

In Helaman 10:4, a time of great stress for Nephi, the voice of the Lord came to him with the following assurances: "Blessed art thou, Nephi, for those things which thou hast done; for I have beheld how thou hast with unwearyingness declared the word, which I have given unto thee, unto this people. And thou has not feared them, and hast sought my will and to keep my commandments."

Who wouldn't want to hear, "Blessed art thou, _____"? Nephi was privileged to hear the voice of the Lord and receive God's highest blessings because he did four things well:

- He served the Lord with "unwearyingness."
- He feared God more than man.
- He sought God's will first and foremost over all worldly competing interests.
- He kept God's commandments faithfully and consistently.

In verse five, Nephi is told what God was going to do for him because he listened and obeyed God's will: "Behold, I will bless thee forever; and I will make thee mighty in word and in deed, in faith and in works; yea even that all things shall be done unto thee according to thy word, for thou shalt not ask that which is contrary to my will."

Nephi's blessing was to receive whatever he asked for. God trusted him to not ask for things that'd be contrary to His will. Could this blessing help with love and marriage? In this one scripture story, we learn what we must do to qualify for answers to prayer and what blessings are available to those who do.

If you read the rest of Helaman 10, you'd see what Nephi did with this new power. First, by the Spirit he warned all his people of the coming consequences of their behavior. Second, to save them from themselves, he took the proactive step of causing a famine so they would be too hungry to kill each other in war. Third, after they had learned their lesson and repented, he took to heart the commandment to show "forth afterwards an increase of love toward him whom thou hast reproved, lest he esteem thee to be his enemy." He did this by causing the rain to fall again, ending the drought.

What things would we be inspired to do for our loved ones if we had the prayer power of Nephi? Could we be trusted to only use this power for righteous causes?

Application 9: Praying for a Positive Attitude

Another way that powerful prayer establishes and maintains eternal relationships is by keeping our attitudes about our eternal mates positive and uplifting.

There's a story in Native American lore of an Indian chief who told his tribe one night that there were two dogs inside his mind. One was a white dog that was good, obedient, noble, and courageous. The other was a red dog that was rebellious, snarled, mean spirited, vengeful, and spiteful. He told the tribe the dogs were fighting to the death. One tribe member, not able to wait for the end, asked, "Which one of them will win?" The chief responded, "The one I feed."

The red dog is our natural man tendency to see the worst in others. If undisciplined, it leads us to thoughts about and behaviors toward others that showcase jealousy, resentment, selfishness, and anger. The white dog represents our divine nature and destined Christlike character that must be developed through discipline and hard work. It is the "thou shalt love thy neighbor as thyself" (D&C 59:6) part of our behavior. It is the part that forgives others rather than seeking revenge and prays for those that spitefully use us rather than slandering them in return. The white dog edifies and uplifts, controlling its thoughts and tongue.

The white dog is optimistic and hopes for the best. One of my favorite white dog stories of optimism, faith, and prayer is the story of King Lamoni and his queen. The king was passed out for several days during his conversion process and his advisors thought he was dead and beginning to stink. His wife, the queen, kept a positive attitude: "Therefore, if this is the case, I would that ye should go in and see my husband, for he has been laid upon his bed for the space of two days and two nights; and some say that he is not dead, but others say that he is dead and that he stinketh, and that he ought to be placed in the sepulchre; but as for myself, to me he doth not stink" (Alma 19:5). A positive and prayerful attitude of faith can even change what we smell! It's possible to decide for ourselves each day whether our partner does or "doth not stink."

The rest of the story reads, "And Ammon said unto her: Blessed art thou because of thy exceeding faith; I say unto thee, woman, there has not been such great faith among all the people of the Nephites. And it came to pass that she watched over the bed of her husband, from that time even until that time on the morrow which Ammon had appointed that he should rise. And it came to pass that he arose, according to the words of Ammon; and as he arose, he stretched forth his hand unto the woman, and said: Blessed be the name of God, and blessed art thou" (Alma 19:10–12).

I believe it's difficult to keep a red dog–like spirit of contention, bitterness, anger, and jealousy with us when we pour out our hearts in humble, powerful prayer for our loved ones. The proper spirit will soften and heal our hearts in the process of doing so and we can find peace and pure love for our eternal mate again.

The power of prayer is shown in the rest of Alma 19. Ammon's father, Mosiah, had prayed and been told that Ammon would not be harmed on his dangerous mission to the Lamanites. God fulfilled his promise by striking down an assassin as he tried to murder Ammon. The incident is summarized as follows: "Now we see that Ammon could not be slain, for the Lord had said unto Mosiah, his father: I will spare him, and it shall be unto him according to thy faith—therefore, Mosiah trusted him unto the Lord" (Alma 19:23).

Good things can happen when we trust our loved ones *unto the Lord* by keeping a faith-filled, optimistic, and uplifting attitude about our eternal companion.

Summary

In this chapter, we looked at four things that help prayers to be effective. Prayers should be addressed to the Father in Christ's name, our intents and desires should be the same as Christ's, we should ask for things that are right in God's eyes, and we should refrain from prayers that originate in selfish, unrighteous desires.

Powerful prayer can help find an eternal mate, soften the hearts of loved ones, and help us to know what things to say and do (and to not say and do) to strengthen intimate relationships. God is "mighty to save," being able to perform mighty miracles in our behalf. He wants to hear from us. We are encouraged to pray for righteous goals, responsibilities, and our everyday needs. Following Enos's example, when our own lives are in order, then we can move to the next step of prayer, which is to pray for our immediate loved ones, and then our enemies. It's even more important to do this if our immediate loved ones have become enemies in our minds. Prayer has the power to restore order.

We pray for our loved one's needs and do so especially when they are not acting with love toward us. Sometimes those who spitefully use you and persecute you live in the same house as you. Praying for them will do more good than nagging, seeking revenge, or slandering them. That which we should pray for most is the power and guidance of the Holy Ghost. Learning to perceive and respond to the promptings of the Spirit will make us better listeners in all our mortal relationships.

Finally, powerful prayer helps us feed only the white dog. The white dog represents thoughts and actions that edify and uplift. Prayer can help us control our thoughts, words, anger, and actions. Prayer feeds the white dog, who is always optimistic, cheerful, under control, and hopes for the best. Prayer helps starve the red dog of negative hate, envy, jealousy, anger, and pessimism.

The Principle of Prayer Self-Evaluation Questions

- Do you pray often enough and are your prayers in tune with God's will?
- Do you have enough faith in God, who is "mighty to save," to consistently ask for those the things you need to do to establish or maintain an eternal marriage and family?

- Have you thought about and researched your loved one's needs enough to know the things you should pray about for him or her?
- Can and do you pray for those who spitefully use you and persecute you instead of returning the persecution?
- What have you done this week to help qualify for the guidance of the Holy Ghost? Was it enough?
- How well do you perceive and listen to the Spirit as God attempts to communicate with you? What time of day do these communications come? What can you do to increase the their frequency? Do you record these communications?
- How would you rate your positive attitude about marriage this week on a scale of 1–10, with 10 being the highest?

Chapter 3: Repentance

Successful marriages and families are established and maintained on the principle of repentance.

Understanding the Repentance Principle

Repentance is a Greek word that denotes a change of mind or a fresh perspective. It's a change of direction that leads us toward seeking to emulate God's character traits and His goals for us while striving for our divine destiny and becoming one with God.

Humans are the only sentient beings capable of agency, of morally evaluating behavior, and of repentance. Only we can step outside of ourselves and objectively look at our actions and motives. Only people, with the light of Christ as our guide, can know the difference between right and wrong and alter behavior and desires based upon perceptions of morality. It's what makes us human. Without these, we would not be capable of pure love, eternal marriage, and family relationships.

Practical Applications of the Repentance Principle in Finding and Keeping Eternal Love

Repentance helps establish and maintain eternal relationships in several ways: it gives us the right attitude for finding the right one, mistakes need not be permanent, repentance can stop weaknesses from killing relationships, and repentance can change weaknesses into strengths.

Application 1: The Right Attitude for Finding the Right One

When single and seeking to establish a successful marriage and family, repentance helps us to look for a relationship while having the correct attitude and perspective. So many singles today spend their days searching for the "perfect companion" and make lists of the attributes they hope to find in a perfect match for them. This is not entirely undesirable or unproductive; we need to examine those we date and court. However, there is something even more important that we should focus on in our pursuit of a perfect companion.

The principle of repentance causes us to focus on our own contribution to our relationships and on our own worthiness to show love rather than spending all our time worrying about someone else's degree of perfection. Our judgments, assessments, and criticisms tend to look inward rather than outward to the behaviors of others. The principle of repentance motivates us to make a list of such questions as, "Am I temple worthy? Am I ready for an eternal commitment? Is my relationship with God where it needs to be? Am I worthy of the inspiration of the Holy Ghost? Do I physically present myself the best I can? What do I have to offer someone as an eternal companion? Where can I improve?"

Remember Alma 32 and the development of faith and love from chapter one? "And now, behold, are ye sure that this is a good seed? I say unto you, Yea; for every seed bringeth forth unto its own likeness" (Alma 32:31). It's simple—if you want a nearly perfect mate, use the principle of repentance to become more perfect yourself. The second step in that perfection process, right after faith, is repentance.

Application 2: Mistakes Need Not Be Permanent

The Atonement, with its principle of repentance, makes it possible for individuals to overcome and be forgiven for all sins, both large and small, that can stress intimate relationships and marriages. What would it be like for us to never be able to recover from our sins and be cut off forever from the presence of God and our family in the next life? 2 Nephi 9:8–9 make it clear we'd become subject to Satan and remain in our sins with no hope of escaping that sorry state.

Before serving in Vietnam, my wife and I owned a home in Salt Lake City that we rented out while I served in the military. I grew tired of dealing with renters from a distance and decided to sell the home and buy another one when I got out of the service. My father advised me against it. We had purchased the home in the Holladay area of Salt Lake for $32,000 in 1969 and someone offered to buy it for $36,000 in 1971. I made the mistake of not listening to my father, sold the house, and took the profits and put them in the bank.

We learned a hard lesson about hyperinflation when we moved back to Salt Lake City in 1974 and looked to buy another home. My $36,000 home in Holladay became worth over $70,000, and I couldn't come close to buying another home comparable to it with the $36,000 I had from the 1971 sale. We had to buy a much less desirable and smaller home.

Over the years, that home in Holladay has continued to appreciate until the last time I looked at it—over $600,000. Every year, I looked at how much that home's value increased and realized that my financial mistake got bigger every year.

I'm thankful there is a way to stop the increasing losses in regards to the spiritual and relationship mistakes we make. They don't have to remain with us year after year with the consequences continuing to grow. There is a way to start over and fix the messes. It's repentance, one of the most important principles of a successful marriage because we are all going make mistakes sooner or later and we need to be able to fix them.

The great plan of happiness explains the principle of repentance succinctly: "Behold, he who has repented of his sins, the same is forgiven, and I, the Lord, remember them no more" (D&C 58:42). An understanding of this doctrine can bless a marriage or dating relationship in which sin has led to contention and disunity. Through the doctrine of the Atonement and the principle of repentance, we can be reconciled to God after making mistakes, which makes it possible for the Spirit to return and help restore love and trust in our relationships.

Unfortunately, there is an obstacle to our using the Atonement to receive forgiveness for our sins and becoming clean before the Lord and our partner again. Satan knows sins destroy relationships and thus does all he can to keep us from repenting. He has two great deceptions that can destroy the effects of the Atonement in our lives.

First, he does not want us to know the great magnitude of God's love and His capacity to forgive. Second, he wants us to think that our sins are so bad that we've alienated ourselves from God forever. He often does this by causing us to think it is possible to use up our allotted number of repentance tries for a particular type of sin.

I saw these deceptions working first hand in Vietnam nearly every day. Some LDS soldiers I met had committed serious sins, the most common being sexual sins. Many of our soldiers realized the magnitude of their mistakes and sought repentance. Others were so ashamed of their behavior that they lost any hope of regaining salvation. They were certain God could not love them and developed an attitude of, "Oh well, I'm going to hell so I might as well try to enjoy it." They then went off the deep end of sin and onto illegal activities.

I met several of these young men while visiting soldiers incarcerated in the Long Binh stockade (also known as LBJ, for Long Binh Jail). Their stories had a similar pattern. These prisoners had been drafted, many of them right after getting home from their missions. They failed to stand strong against intense temptations and peer pressure and committed serious sexual sins. Next came depression, failure to repent, loss of faith in God, and avoiding the Church and fellow LDS soldiers.

Next came a way to forget all this by taking heroin, which seemed to be used by everyone they knew. Addiction came quickly because of the strength of the drug, which was grown in northern Vietnam, shipped down the Ho Chi Minh trail, and sold to and marketed by the South Vietnamese mafia. Our deceived soldiers soon found their appetite for heroin far exceeded their ability to pay for it, so they resorted to stealing whatever they could and selling the items on the black market in Saigon. It seemed to me that participating LDS soldiers were inexperienced thieves and always got caught.

It was a sad thing to watch a two hundred-pound soldier wither away to nearly a hundred pounds from his addiction to heroin. His soul seemed to fade along with his body. I spent most of my time as an army chaplain in Vietnam, counseling with these solders addicted to heroin. Of all those our medical staff and I tried to help, the only ones I observed who were able to beat this demon were those who turned back to God for strength by using the eternal principle of repentance. There is a reason why the first step of all twelve-step recovery programs is to admit we are powerless before the addiction and to turn our problems over to God.

In Vietnam, I saw what worked and what didn't work in defeating addiction. Those who returned to God and followed the steps to repentance, whether they were LDS or of another faith, could beat it; those who didn't were beaten down by it.

Application 3: Repentance Can Stop Weaknesses from Destroying Relationships

The repentance aspect of the Atonement blesses a marriage or dating relationship by giving us the power to overcome weaknesses of the flesh, both small and great, that have the potential to destroy such relationships.

There are many things that need to be repented of, that can destroy our ability to find and keep true love. At the top of the list is pride and its first cousin, selfishness. Is it even possible to count the many ways there are to exhibit pride and selfishness in intimate relationships?

If pride and selfishness have crept into our personalities and are destroying our ability to form and keep intimate relationships, there is hope. We can change, even after we have failed to do so time and again. God won't give up on us, so why should we?

The Spirit taught Alma, "Yea, and as often as my people repent will I forgive them their trespasses against me" (Mosiah 26:30). Would Jesus Christ actually do that for someone like you and me, even though we've relapsed many times? Absolutely.

Our Redeemer knows what we need and how to take care of our mistakes—"even Jesus Christ, your advocate, who knoweth the weakness of man and how to succor them who are tempted" (D&C 62:1). To succor is to go to the aid of one in distress and bring relief. There is no greater source of succor to sinners than that provided by our Lord and Savior.

In addition to the pride and selfishness already mentioned, there is a long list of relationship-killing weaknesses tempting us today. A few of the more common ones are anger, abuse, alcohol, drug abuse (both prescription and illegal), pornography in all its forms, materialism, gaming or sports addictions, laziness, forgetting God, and becoming a law unto ourselves.

Moroni wrote of the behavior he saw in our times, and he was not complimentary: "Yea, it shall come in a day when there shall be great pollutions upon the face of the earth; there shall be murders, and robbing, and lying, and deceivings, and whoredoms, and all manner of abominations; when there shall be many who will say, Do this, or do that, and it mattereth not, for the Lord will uphold such at the last day. But wo unto such, for they are in the gall of bitterness and in the bonds of iniquity" (Mormon 8:31).

Application 4: Repentance Can Change Weaknesses into Strengths

"And if men come unto me I will show unto them their weakness. I give unto men weakness that they may be humble; and my grace is sufficient for all men that humble themselves before me; for if they humble themselves before me, and have faith in me, then will I make weak things become strong unto them" (Ether 12:27).

Ether 12:27 is the Lord's promise that our weaknesses, if repented of and defeated, can be transformed into strengths. It is a wonderful promise of hope that lives can be transformed and relationships and marriages saved. People can change if properly motivated (and for the right reasons).

As mentioned above, there are many addictive weaknesses of the flesh that destroy true love today. Their seductive powers destroy potential relationships from ever forming and eternal marriages from lasting.

Alma the Younger's advice to his son Shiblon shows us the relationship between our ability to offer someone pure love and our ability to control our passions: "and also see that ye bridle all your passions, that ye may be filled with love; see that ye refrain from idleness" (Alma 38:12). Basically, if we can't control our passions, we can never be filled with pure, eternal love.

Addictive weaknesses of the flesh destroy relationships in many ways. I mention only two here. First, they make the addict unworthy of receiving, from God, the gift of pure love for another. Moroni teaches that love is "bestowed upon all who are true followers of his Son, Jesus Christ" (Moroni 7:48). Without bridling our passions, we cannot show pure love for another because our selfishness leads us to think only of our own perceived and excessive needs. The needs of others become a casualty to our passions.

The Apostle Paul puts it this way: "Stand fast therefore in the liberty wherewith Christ hath made us free, and be not entangled again with the yoke of bondage (Galatians 5:1). "This I say then, Walk in the Spirit, and ye shall not fulfil the lust of the flesh. For the flesh lusteth against the Spirit, and the Spirit against the flesh: and these are contrary the one to the other: so that ye cannot do the things that ye would" (Galatians 5:16–17). Sin is "a yoke of bondage" that drives the Spirit away and causes us to fall far short of our potential so that we "cannot do the things that ye would."

Second, weaknesses and addictions destroy others' faith in the addict, making it difficult to show love for him or her. The principle of repentance and the possibility that our weaknesses can be turned into strengths can solve both these problems.

As addicts develop faith in the grace of Christ and learn to be humble, they come to understand that the evil monster that leaves them with such low opinions of themselves after each episode is not all-powerful and can be defeated. This knowledge leads them to believe in themselves and desire to have their weakness replaced with the strengths that can lead them to become winners instead of losers.

The partners of addicts also need to develop faith in the process and realize that these damaged individuals don't have to remain that way. We are all repairable and capable of being whole again. The principle of repentance can restore our faith in humanity and the Lord's ability to turn weaknesses into strengths. The scriptures have many examples of this in action. The Apostle Paul in the New Testament heard a voice and saw a light that changed his life forever. His weakness in sin was turned into a mighty strength in the Lord.

Alma the Elder repented from being one of King Noah's wicked priests and became a mighty prophet of God and founder of the Church among the Nephites. Alma the Younger was, along with the sons of Mosiah, the "vilest of sinners" (Mosiah 28:4). All of these mighty men repented of their sinful ways and turned their considerable talents into strengths, which the Lord used to build His kingdom.

These scriptural examples demonstrate that any of us can change and become a new person in the Lord with the strength to perform mighty deeds.

Summary

In this chapter, we reviewed how the principle of repentance helps us form and sustain eternal relationships. *Repentance* is a Greek word that denotes a change of mind or a fresh view about God, about oneself, or about the world. Repentance takes us away from worldliness and toward emulating the character of God.

We discussed four ways the principle of repentance helps us find and keep true love. First, repentance leads us to a proper attitude for finding the right one. It causes us first to look inward at our own imperfections and motivates us to seek higher goals. As we reach these higher goals, the right one is more likely to be attracted to us both before and after marriage.

Second, it's important to realize our mistakes need not be permanent. The plan of salvation allows us to learn from experiences and grow from the process. It can create or restore unity, love, and trust in relationships if ever weakened by sin.

Third, repentance helps us overcome and stop any of the many weaknesses of the flesh that destroy relationships. Repentance is the most important step any of us can perform when we seek to reclaim our lives and stop hurting those we love the most.

Fourth, repentance leads the way in changing our weaknesses into strengths. The energy and expense it takes to feed a lust of the flesh can be sublimated, or redirected, to productive activities and worthwhile goals.

The Principle of Repentance Self-Evaluation Questions

- Do your judgments, assessments, and criticisms tend to look inward rather than outward to the behaviors of others?
- Do you expect more from others than you do from yourself?
- Is your level of physical, social, spiritual, and character development complete enough to attract others to you? Have you taken the talents and gifts the Lord has given you in these areas and added to them?
- When you make a mistake that offends God and those you love, do you immediately seek repentance and take the steps to assure it will not happen again?

- Do you regularly take time to evaluate your behavior and determine if you have any weaknesses that are negatively impacting those you love?
- When repenting of a bad habit, do you actively look for positive, productive things to do that fill the void caused by stopping the harmful behavior?

Chapter 4: Forgiveness

Successful marriages and families are established and maintained on the principle of forgiveness.

Understanding the Forgiveness Principle

The principle of forgiveness in courtship and marriage follows the dictionary definition closely. Courtship and marriage relationships frequently put us in need of practicing the *act of forgiving*, or finding ourselves in a *state of being forgiven*. No one is capable of interacting with another person in an intimate relationship without sooner or later failing to meet his or her expectations in some way. Without the ability to just let it go and to stop harboring hurt feelings, it's nearly impossible to form an eternal marriage or keep on going. Many of us need to work on improving our disposition or willingness to forgive.

The scriptures set the standard for what is expected of us as to our disposition or willingness to forgive. Becoming comfortable in a relationship before marriage or actually getting married does not negate the obligation we all have to forgive men and women of their trespasses against us:

- "And forgive us our debts, as we forgive our debtors" (Matthew 6:12).
- "For if ye forgive men their trespasses, your heavenly Father will also forgive you: But if ye forgive not men their trespasses,

neither will your Father forgive your trespasses" (Matthew 6:14–15).

- "Take heed to yourselves: If thy brother trespass against thee, rebuke him; and if he repent, forgive him. And if he trespass against thee seven times in a day, and seven times in a day turn again to thee, saying, I repent; thou shalt forgive him" (Luke 17:3–4).
- "And it came to pass that I did frankly forgive them all that they had done" (1 Nephi 7:21).
- "Behold, he who has repented of his sins, the same is forgiven, and I, the Lord, remember them no more" (D&C 58:42).
- "Wherefore, I say unto you, that ye ought to forgive one another; for he that forgiveth not his brother his trespasses standeth condemned before the Lord; for there remaineth in him the greater sin" (D&C 64:8–9).
- "I, the Lord, will forgive whom I will forgive, but of you it is required to forgive all men" (D&C 64:10).
- "Verily, verily, I say unto you, my servants, that inasmuch as you have forgiven one another your trespasses, even so I, the Lord, forgive you" (D&C 82:1).

Practical Applications of the Forgiveness Principle in Finding and Keeping True Love

Applying the principle of forgiveness helps us to establish and maintain eternal relationships in a number of ways, three of which will be discussed here.

Application 1: The Principle of Forgiveness Can Help Us Not Lose a Good Eternal Mate

I recall one young lady who was engaged to a handsome BYU graduate, who was a returned missionary with a professional job. She asked him one day on the phone—as he was working out of town— if he had ever had a problem with pornography. There was a long pause on the other end of the line and she felt her heart sink.

He explained that in high school he became addicted to pornography for a year and had to work with his bishop for the next two years to beat the addiction. His repentance complete, he enrolled in

BYU and later served an honorable mission. He returned to BYU, graduated, and went on to earn a graduate degree. He never relapsed from high school to the time he met her (a period of nearly ten years) and reported that he was still clean and intended to stay that way for the rest of his life.

Despite his being clean for ten years, the young woman couldn't get the idea of his looking at and lusting over pornographic images out of her mind. It haunted her, destroyed her peace, and brought her to the brink of calling off the wedding.

In theory, the young lady should have understood that her fiancé was fully worthy of taking her to the temple because his repentance had stood the test of time. The scriptures are clear on this: "Behold, he who has repented of his sins, the same is forgiven, and I, the Lord, remember them no more" (D&C 58:42). In reality, it still upset her. She needed help letting it go and accepting him for what he really was: a repentant, reborn saint worthy of a temple recommend and of her.

Fortunately, this story has a happy ending because she allowed the Savior to take the burden from her. However, I've seen other couples over the years that could not let it go, their inability to achieve a disposition or unwillingness to forgive, costing them the opportunity to form an eternal union with someone they could've been happy with.

I've listened to many such stories over the years in my marriage classes and in counseling settings. It's always a difficult situation when you discover the person you love has "a past" that you're disappointed with. I have a lesson where I ask my students if they would still marry someone who had been in a sexual relationship with another person.

I've asked literally thousands of students this over the years and their answers usually fall into one of two categories: The majority agree that even though it would be difficult, if they truly loved the person, they would find a way to forgive him or her and move forward. They often cite several of the scriptures listed previously.

A minority of the students says they would forgive the person and wish him or her well, but they would not want to marry him or her. These students give a variety of reasons for this personal decision. Ideally, the best situation is for both partners to follow the Lord's plan of happiness and wait for marriage before sexual relationships. Realistically, many have fallen in this corrupt world, but none are irredeemable to the Lord. The twin principles of repentance and forgiveness have the potential to heal all mistakes of this nature.

I recall a close friend's story of how his eternal marriage nearly ended before the wedding. His fiancée revealed to him one week before the wedding day that she had over $25,000 in student loans. Some of you reading this may not think that is all that much money for student loans today. However, this was in 1968, and the comparable inflation value in 2015 is $173,165.

My friend spent the next three days in prayer, as well as fasting and attending the temple, trying to decide if he wanted to be saddled with this burden. Finally, he decided she was worth it and moved forward in faith with the wedding.

Application 2: The Principle of Forgiveness
Helps Us Keep an Eternal Marriage Eternal

Forgiveness in marriage on a day-to-day basis is about patience more than anything else. Patience is an unnatural yet cherished act and earned virtue. It is indispensible to finding a love that we will be happy with throughout all eternity. Merriam-Webster defines *patient* as:

- bearing pains or trials calmly or without complaint
- manifesting forbearance under provocation or strain
- not hasty or impetuous
- steadfast despite opposition, difficulty, or adversity
- (a) able or willing to bear—used with *of* (what is your level of forbearance before you become a little negative?)
- (b) susceptible, admitting

The price of failing to develop patience is described in two scripture passages. The first is Mosiah 2:32–33, where a "wo" is placed upon all those have an inability to be "steadfast despite opposition, difficulty, or adversity" and will take this lack of everyday patience with them to the other side of the veil. King Benjamin didn't directly call this *wo* a lack of patience, but rather called it an evil spirit of contention. Contention is often caused by being hasty and impetuous, not to mention failing to forbear under provocation or strain. It appears that this evil spirit spoken of by King Benjamin, if allowed to go unchecked, has the power to define and mold our personalities and consume our lives: "But, O my people, beware lest there shall arise contentions among you, and ye list to obey the evil spirit, which was spoken of by my father Mosiah. For behold, there is a wo pronounced upon him who listeth to obey that spirit; for if he listeth to obey him, and remaineth and dieth in his sins, the same drinketh damnation to his own soul; for he receiveth for his wages an everlasting punishment, having transgressed the law of God contrary to his own knowledge" (Mosiah 2:32–33).

This is actually a shocking scripture if we look at it carefully. Does it say that someone who has a habit of being contentious at the time of his or her death is in danger of damning his or her own soul because of this habit? This sounds like a heavy price for being an impatient cynic. Is it possible to be so pessimistic in our view of people that we end up training our brain to "obey that spirit" whether we want it to or not? Is there actually a "law of God" that cautions us not to be overly contentious, arguable, debatable, litigious, and touchy? I believe the answers are yes, yes, and yes. I believe God is a positive person and expects us to be positive in our outlooks in day-to-day living.

We act with contention and an evil spirit toward loved ones when we fail to forgive them of simple, everyday behavior we don't like. We risk constantly and repeatedly losing patience with them until it becomes habit. Without the relationship-saving restraint of patience and the ability to forgive on the spot, we proceed, over and over again, to deem them guilty of offenses and quickly become their judge, jury, and executioner every day that we interact with them.

There are so many ways to dish out punishment to someone whom we allow to offend us. There's sarcasm and put-downs, gossiping, and exaggerating faults. We easily ignore any good they do or have ever done. We can constantly criticize and nag them—and then escalate to using contemptuous language (which constitutes verbal abuse). We can disrespect their opinions on any subjects without even really listening to them. How natural it becomes to give them the cold shoulder and to withhold all affection from them for long periods of time. Our lack of respect for them grows to the point that we just walk away from them (stonewalling) when they try to discuss something important with us. If Satan gets a complete hold on our hearts, we could take it to the next level with physical or sexual abuse, or try to punish our spouses through adultery. These are but a few of the "evil spirit" tools routinely used by those of us who lack the patience and the capacity to quickly forgive each other for less-than-pleasant everyday interactions.

In the second scripture showing the price for failing to develop patience, Alma explained clearly what happens in the end to each habitual, self-conditioned cynic:

> Ye cannot say, when ye are brought to that awful crisis, that I will repent, that I will return to my God. Nay, ye cannot say this; *for that same spirit which doth possess your bodies at the time that ye go out of this life, that same spirit will have power to possess your body in that eternal world.* For behold, if ye have procrastinated the day of your repentance even until death, behold, ye have become subjected to the spirit of the devil, and he doth seal you his; therefore, the Spirit of the Lord hath withdrawn from you, and hath no place in you, and the devil hath all power over you; and this is the final state of the wicked. (Alma 34:34–35; emphasis added)

I have a friend whose mother-in-law passed away and the family found a set of journals she kept for the last thirty years of her life. The surviving family members divided them up and each read one and reported on what was found.

They all discovered the same kind of writing. Apparently whenever someone—usually a family member—offended her (which was nearly every day), she wrote her bitter feelings in these journals. They included such observations as, "Susan made a long-distance phone call on my phone today and did not offer to pay for it. She is so inconsiderate." "Bill and Martha's Christmas present this year was so tacky and cheap. I know they could have afforded more but it's obvious they care about no one but themselves." There were no positive comments about anyone in the journals.

Shortly after the funeral, the family members voted to burn the journals. If anyone reading this book keeps such a record, I suggest you save your family members the trouble and burn it before your own funeral.

Again, have we allowed the natural man to take advantage of our lack of patience, possibly starting with our spouse or those closest to us? Instead of learning pure love, have we learned impure contempt?

Instead of learning to love God first and foremost by learning to love mankind (Matthew 22), have we allowed our lack of patience to turn us into bitter disparagers?

If we wander down this forbidden path of hate and dismay, we risk setting ourselves up for being unhappy for the rest of eternity. It's a dangerous and slippery slope that should be avoided, and we all have the choice of letting them go or hanging onto life's injustices and feeding those bitter feelings until all our molehills explode into fully mature mountains of "evil spirit" behavior.

Application 3: The Principle of Forgiveness Can Help Keep a Marriage Eternal—Even after a Terrorist Attack

I recall a friend telling me about her devastating marriage breakup. She said it came as a complete surprise to her after several decades of marriage. She wondered how another woman could invade her sacred home and legally steal her most valuable treasure: her husband. She said if the invader had stolen anything else in the home—all of which were far less valuable to her—the thief could be arrested; but apparently her husband was considered fair game in today's "open-minded," morally relative world. I call this type of behavior a terrorist attack. It conveys the idea of a surprise attack from outside hostile forces seeking to better their lives at the expense of yours. I am not implying, however, that in this story the husband could not have resisted such an attack if he had practiced caution and discipline and if he were more committed to honoring his marriage covenants.

When my friend confronted her husband and his mistress about how they could justify such behavior, they both shrugged and replied that they had not planned on it, but that it had "just happened." My friend replied they should have known that if they got on the freeway that leads to Los Angeles and they chose to stay on that freeway, mile after mile, they would eventually arrive in L.A. It shouldn't have been a surprise.

Nearly all marriages begin with the expectation of exclusivity— that is, there will be no sexual relations of any kind with anyone else, period. It's not hard to understand this basic expectation. However, I've seen many people, some who believe in God and His teachings about exclusivity and others who claim there is no God, fall into adultery. They all start off thinking they are an exception to this law and act accordingly. My experience in dealing with them in a counseling setting is that they never find lasting happiness.

Despite Hollywood's attempts to depict adultery and hedonism as natural human behavior with little to no consequences, I have thousands of hours of counseling case notes that scream, "It's a lie!" Our Heavenly Father warns us, "Wickedness never was happiness" (Alma 41:10). It never has been and it never will be.

Latter-day Saints who wander on this forbidden path quickly learn they're walking in a minefield. Unlike a minefield, it isn't *if* you are going to get blown up; it's more like *when*. Sometimes the damage is too extensive to recover from and the marriage is over. Other times the wanderer comes to his or her senses, retraces his or her steps backward out of the minefield of adultery, and then tries to repair the damage. It is in this situation that the twin principles of repentance and forgiveness have the power to heal broken hearts and marriages.

I often ask my marriage students which is harder: to be the sinner seeking repentance or to be the innocent victim or offended spouse that is being asked to find a way to forgive the wayward mate. My observation is that neither role is any fun, and both require gut-wrenching courage, determination, and a gargantuan test of faith.

Years ago, I worked with an LDS couple on the verge of divorce. The husband was angry and not responsive to counseling while the wife was bewildered, sad, and trying to save the marriage. The husband had a list of things he was unhappy about. He was upset about her weight, even though she'd given birth to several children and couldn't have been more than twenty pounds over her ideal weight. He had other issues with her, but all of them seemed just as frivolous.

One week, the wife made two startling discoveries. First, she uncovered a plan by her husband to take her name off their house, cars, savings accounts, and retirement funds. He was trying to transfer all their major assets into the name of someone she didn't know. If that were not bad enough, she found a company newsletter from her husband's work that announced his engagement to a coworker. Apparently, he forgot to tell his girlfriend that he was married and his wife that he had a girlfriend.

With these revelations, the woman turned to friends and relatives for advice. They all told her to see a lawyer quickly and protect herself and her children from this "terrorist attack." She went to the temple and then to a lawyer.

While she was filling out some paperwork at the lawyer's office, the prompting came to her that this was all wrong. Her husband's behavior was wrong and her reaction to it was wrong, so she needed to try something else. She didn't know what to do, but she got in her car and started driving. Eventually, she drove to her husband's work.

While in the parking lot, it came to her that she should go inside and challenge him. She got out of the car, stormed into his office, and confronted him with the evidence of his deception. She encouraged him to repent and save himself from any further damage to his soul. She told him if he did this immediately, she would forgive him and they could save their marriage and family. To everyone's surprise, he seemed relieved and agreed to seek repentance. She forgave him and they remained married.

How many marriages struck by a terrorist attack like this could've been saved—and the unavoidable train of consequences of divorce avoided—if the offended spouse had been able to develop a "disposition or willingness to forgive"? I certainly realize that sometimes it's best for a marriage to end, but more often it's not. These are difficult decisions that must be carefully made. President James E. Faust gives some of the best advice I've read concerning whether to seek divorce or to forgive and work it out:

> What, then, might be "just cause" for breaking the covenants of marriage? Over a lifetime of dealing with human problems, I have struggled to understand what might be considered "just cause" for breaking of covenants. I confess I do not claim the wisdom or authority to definitively state what is "just cause." Only the parties to the marriage can determine this. They must bear the responsibility for the train of consequences which inevitably follow if these covenants are not honored. In my opinion, "just cause" should be nothing less serious than a prolonged and apparently irredeemable relationship which is destructive of a person's dignity as a human being.
>
> At the same time, I have strong feelings about what is not provocation for breaking the sacred covenants of marriage. Surely it is not simply "mental distress," nor "personality differences," nor having "grown apart,"

nor having "fallen out of love." This is especially so where there are children. ("Father, Come Home," *Ensign*, May 1993, 36–37)

Here are some questions to consider before seeking a divorce: If you stay in the relationship, will it harm your dignity as a human being? Has there been enough time for your reconciliation attempts to qualify as "prolonged" and is the relationship "apparently irredeemable"? If you choose to stay in the marriage, will you and your children be emotionally and physically safe?

As President Faust taught, "Only the parties to the marriage can determine this." I do feel, however, that each of us will have to stand before our Maker and answer for how hard we tried to make our marriage eternal and thus qualify for all the rights and privileges that are bestowed upon the faithful. How forgiving do we have to be? I refer you to the scriptures on forgiveness at the beginning of this chapter.

Application 4: The Principle of Forgiveness Can Help Us Find Peace after a Failed Relationship

A student of mine from Russia told me the following story about how the spirit of forgiveness helped prepare her for meeting the missionaries and eventually marrying for time and all eternity and coming to America:

> My first marriage lasted five years. It was not a healthy relationship from the start. My ex-husband was abusive, physically and verbally, and since I had observed this type of family life quite frequently growing up, I assumed that this was normal in married life. I naïvely hoped things would change for the better because I was attractive, a great homemaker, had a well-paying job while still attending college, and was willing to compromise. But instead of getting better, my marriage got worse. No amount of effort and good will can win against someone who refuses to give up addictions like alcohol and pornography. It took me some time after the divorce to come to the realization that I couldn't move on with my life and return to my normally happy self if I could not forgive my former spouse of all of the abuse that my daughter and I went through. In the early 1990s in Russia, after Perestroika, the entire country was on rations. After I filed for divorce, my ex cleaned out our entire bank account and stole every piece of furniture and

ounce of clothing my daughter and I had, which brought us well below
the poverty line. Despite all of that, I was willing to forgive and forget.
I wanted to move on.

I forgave him for all the nightmares that my child still vividly
remembers. In fact, when my mother or my daughter remind me of
the terrible things that they still remember, I oftentimes can't recall
them. However, I clearly remember the day when I made the decision
to forgive and move on. I remember the feeling of complete happiness
and joy. It felt like a huge weight fell off my shoulders. I felt free when
I looked at my empty flat (he even took the light switches) and despite
the tears I was laughing happily because I knew I was going to start my
life all over again. I felt like I finally turned the page and the new one
was crispy clean and ready for me to write my new story. And that story
was going to be great and fun, just the way I always wanted it to be.
Though I forgave, there are some things that are hard to forget. I strive
hard not to dwell on my past but oftentimes it is just beyond my
ability to do so. I am so glad I know and believe in Christ's infinite
Atonement and God's love for all of His children. This knowledge
gives me power to continue to forgive and heal.

Roadblocks to Forgiveness

Here are three of the many types of remarks I've heard over the
years that can effectively block any chance for compassion, forgiveness,
and hope of reconciliation:

1. "What if I get burned again if I take him or her back? I don't
know if I can go through that again." Many a victim of adultery
or other types of terrorist attacks have asked this question. C. S.
Lewis looked at it this way:

> To love at all is to be vulnerable. Love anything, and your heart will
> certainly be wrung and possibly be broken. If you want to make
> sure of keeping it intact, you must give your heart to no one, not
> even to an animal. Wrap it carefully round with hobbies and little
> luxuries; avoid all entanglements; lock it up safe in the casket or
> coffin of your selfishness. But in that casket—safe, dark, motion-
> less, airless—it will change. It will not be broken; it will become
> unbreakable, impenetrable, irredeemable . . . the only place outside
> Heaven where you can be perfectly safe from all the dangers . . . of
> love is Hell" (C. S. Lewis, *The Four Loves*, 111).

2. "How can I ever trust him (or her) again? The marriage can never be the same. I just can't let it go and forgive!" President James E. Faust in the October 2001 general conference gave the following counsel: "The Atonement not only benefits the sinner but also benefits those sinned against—that is, the victims. By forgiving 'those who trespass against us' (JST, Matthew 6:13) the Atonement brings a measure of peace and comfort to those who have been innocently victimized by the sins of others." Please read his entire address if you are experiencing this roadblock.

3. "It's not fair. No one should be allowed to get away with something as devastating as this. I'm not going to let mercy rob justice." I believe there is one thing about mortality that's absolutely certain, and that is we are all going to get exactly what we deserve when it's finally over. Read Jacob 2:34–35 and 3:1–3. The Lord speaks first to those who are "pure in heart"—the offended and innocent wives in this case. He tells them to "lift up your heads and receive the pleasing word of God, and feast upon his love." He assures the pure in heart that He will "send down justice upon those who seek your destruction." No one is ever going to rob justice in the end. The scriptures are clear on this topic. The question is, do we have the faith to believe the scriptures, trust God, and let go of the bitterness?

There is no need to be a vigilante and run down adulterous offenders. We don't need to allow the seeming unfairness of this life to consume our lives in bitterness and sorrow. The Lord is clear that the adulterer will not get away with anything. Jacob 3:3 states, "But, wo, wo, unto you that are not pure in heart, that are filthy this day before God; for except ye repent the land is cursed for your sakes." Eventually, we are all going to get exactly what we deserve.

Oftentimes, it requires patience for the innocent victim to trust in the Lord's when and where of His justice. I have known several couples where, after a divorce and the appropriate Church discipline for the adulterous partner (not to mention a length of time), the offending spouse was allowed to be rebaptized. The innocent partner became so enraged that the ex-spouse was allowed to repent that the innocent partner left the Church in retaliation. In these types of cases, patience and forgiveness may or may not be able to save a marriage, but they can save the pure in heart from losing their own salvation. It's been said that for those who refuse to forgive and savor their afflictions, it's like drinking poison and waiting for the other person to die.

Summary

Courtship and marriage relationships frequently put us in need of practicing the *act of forgiving* or finding ourselves in a *state of being forgiven*. This chapter examined the importance of increasing our ability to "let it go" and stop harboring hurt feelings. We examined the importance of improving our disposition or willingness to forgive.

This chapter discussed four of the many possible applications of the principle of forgiveness. First, many potentially successful eternal marriages fail because the one or both of the individuals involved had not developed a disposition or willingness to forgive. This includes an inability to forgive mistakes made both before they met and after. Learning to forgive can save us from making mistakes we may regret for the rest of our lives.

Second, the principle of forgiveness helps keep a marriage eternal on a day-to-day basis. Patience is the state of enduring under difficult circumstances and exhibiting forbearance when under strain. Mosiah 2:32 teaches "there is a wo pronounced upon him who listeth to obey that spirit;" that is, the spirit of contention that is most often born of our inability to exhibit tolerance.

Third, the principle of forgiveness can help us survive terrorist attacks on our marriages. The most common type of outside attack on marriage is adultery, but the principle can be applied to a wide variety of potentially terminal mistakes.

Fourth, the principle of forgiveness can help us heal from failed relationships.

Finally, we looked at three different types of roadblocks that inhibit the activation of the healing and relieving powers of forgiveness in our lives.

Principle of Forgiveness Self-Evaluation Questions

- How would you rate your overall disposition or willingness to forgive others?
  A. High—I'm a forgiving person who doesn't hold grudges.
  B. Average—I'm about the same as most people.
  C. Low—I need much improvement in this area.
- How willing are you to forgive the repented past sins of your partner?
  A. High—I'm a forgiving person.
  B. Average—I'm about the same as most people.
  C. Low—I'm not able to do this.
- Generally, I can easily and quickly forgive others who I feel have wronged me.
  A. In nearly all situations.
  B. Most of the time.
  C. Seldom, if ever.
- When confronted with an aggressive, rude driver in traffic . . .
  A. I usually react to their stupidity in a similar manner, as it's important to teach them a lesson.
  B. I'm patient and remain in control of my emotions the vast majority of the time.
- How is your ability to patiently endure under difficult relationship circumstances?
  A. I'm patient in nearly all situations.
  B. Most of the time.
  C. Seldom, if ever.
- Can you persevere (remain calm) in the face of delay or provocation without acting on annoyance or anger in a negative way?
  A. In nearly all situations.
  B. Most of the time.
  C. Seldom, if ever.
- I can easily forgive my loved one for the little annoyances and mistakes he or she makes on a daily basis.
  A. Nearly always.
  B. The majority of the time.

C. I feel he (or she) will never improve without my continually giving feedback and criticism about his (or her) multitude of bad habits, sloppiness, lack of attention to details, bad driving, or social faux pas (awkward blunders).

- If my partner were to make a major mistake in a time of weakness and were to afterward seek proper repentance and also seek forgiveness from me, I would . . .
  A. I would most likely forgive and take him (or her) back.
  B. I might take him (or her) back after sufficient punishment has been given and suffering has occurred.
  C. No, there is no forgiveness for something like that.

- Have you ever or do you think you might ever allow one of the three roadblocks discussed in this chapter to stop you from forgiving a loved one? If so, which one?

Chapter 5: Respect

Successful marriages and families are established and maintained by understanding and correctly applying true principles of respect.

Understanding the Principle of Respect in Intimate Relationships

Respect influences behavior in significant ways. Before discussing the importance of respect in marriage relationships, let's take a look at two examples of the how respect works in basic human interactions.

A professional football player—a famous receiver at that time—stated during a media interview that if his team had a better quarterback (and he recommended someone from another team), their team would be undefeated. This resulted in the receiver being censored and traded to another team. When his former teammate and quarterback was asked later how he felt about the disrespectful remark from his former teammate, he calmly replied that the receiver was entitled to his opinion and that he wished him well with his new team. However, the depth of the quarterback's feelings for being disrespected came out when he added that he had no intention of talking to the receiver again.

His response reminds me of an Old Testament scripture, which read, "A brother offended is harder to be won than a strong city: and their contentions are like the bars of a castle" (Proverbs 18:19).

The second example shows that effects of perceived disrespect can be far more serious than a lost friendship. Several female college students decided to go out for a night of dancing. After, in a joyous mood and talking about their evening while driving home, they hardly noticed when they cut off a car of young men as they changed lanes. Unfortunately, the men were members of a gang who felt the young women had disrespected them. They pulled up to the women at the next stoplight and fired gunshots into their car, killing one and wounding another, before speeding away.

This second example wasn't just an isolated incident. In talking with a friend who is a prison chaplain, I asked him what the most common crime was in the state prison where he worked. He replied, "Murder, in one form or another." He went on to explain that most of them committed these crimes because someone had "dissed" them, or disrespected them in some way to which they'd reacted violently.

Respect is an important element of any human interaction. It's also vital to understand how this works in intimate relationships.

Feeling and *Showing* Respect in Intimate Relationships

American psychologist Abraham Maslow (1908–1970) clarified the importance of respect in intimate relationships.[12] Maslow theorized about human needs and called them our "hierarchy of needs." He laid out five layers of needs that have to be achieved in the following order: First, the physiological needs of air, food, and water. We can't survive for long without these basic essentials. When these are met, we can then focus on our needs for safety and security, found in the second level of stability and protection. Third, when we feel safe enough, we can focus on our innate needs for the third level of love and belonging that are found through such things as having friends, a sweetheart or spouse, children, and a sense of community in a church, gang, or even something like a chess club. When these needs are met, we then progress to the fourth level, which is our need for esteem or respect.

Maslow noted two levels of esteem needs: lower and higher. The lower is the esteem and respect we need from others. This includes things like fame, glory, recognition, status, attention, a good reputation, appreciation, and dignity. The higher level of esteem calls for feelings of self-respect, confidence, competence, independence, achievement, mastery, and freedom.

If esteem or respect is missing in our lives, then we develop low self-esteem and inferiority complexes that cause us great difficulty in forming and keeping intimate relationships. Without at least a little lower level and a somewhat normal higher level of esteem in our lives, we cannot reach the target of perfect love because we aren't capable of progressing to Maslow's fifth and final level of self-actualization (the need to reach our full potential). I believe it is what the great plan of salvation refers to as our "divine destiny." None of us can reach our divine destiny without the ability to intimately become one with an eternal mate (see Doctrine and Covenants 131).

In much of the literature about love both inside and out of the Church, the terms *love* and *respect* are often used together almost as though they are synonyms. "The Family: A Proclamation to the World," however, lists respect separately as one of the nine principles upon which successful marriages and families are established and maintained. The proclamation lists respect before love, and in this chapter I also try to show that respect must come before true love.

Here are five dictionary definitions that help to understand the term *respect* and its close synonym, *esteem*. Notice how often the terms *feel* and *show* are used in the definitions:

- American Heritage Dictionary of the English Language: "To *feel* or *show* deferential regard for; esteem. A *feeling* of appreciative, often deferential regard; esteem. Willingness to show consideration or appreciation."
- Macmillan Dictionary: "A *feeling* of admiration that you have for someone because of their personal qualities, their achievements, or their status, and that you *show* by treating them in a polite and kind way."
- Cambridge Dictionaries Online: "Admiration *felt* or *shown* for someone or something that you believe has good ideas or qualities."
- Webster's New World College Dictionary: "Respect means to *feel* or *show* esteem or honor for someone or something. Other words for esteem: regard, respect, appreciation; see admiration.

To attach a high value to prize, respect, value, hold in high regard; see admire, appreciate."

- Oxford Dictionaries: "A *feeling* of deep admiration for someone or something elicited by their abilities, qualities, or achievements. Admire (someone or something) deeply, as a result of their abilities, qualities, or achievements."

It appears *respect* has at least three meanings when it comes to intimate relationships. First, it is how we feel about ourselves. Do we have the self-esteem and respect for ourselves necessary to feel we have something to offer another person in dating, courtship, or marriage? Do we feel we have what it takes to find a love that will last to eternity? Sometimes life can be unfair and brutal and make us feel like we're damaged goods. Divorced parents, failed relationship attempts, school or business failures, a lack of educational opportunities, abuse, and a multitude of other tragedies or perceived deficiencies can leave us feeling unworthy of love. I will not spend a long time on this aspect of respect but will refer the reader again to 2 Timothy 1:7: "For God hath not given us the spirit of fear; but of power, and of love, and of a sound mind." We all have the ability to rebound after setbacks and can do so by calling upon God's love, support, and ability to not allow our fears to paralyze us. None of us are permanent prisoners of our pasts, and all of us have the ability to increase our self-esteem and respect.

The second way that respect affects intimate relationships has to do with our *feelings* about someone. The third has to do with the kind of behavior we *show* toward them because of these feelings. The rest of this chapter deals with the second and third meanings of respect.

We develop feelings of approval for people based upon their particular combination of abilities, qualities, or achievements. We then naturally show respect for them by treating them in polite, flattering, and otherwise kind ways. Respect means we first have positive *feelings* toward them, and then *show* our respect through our actions.

In intimate relationships, a natural progression of respect occurs. When a mate-seeking boy meets an eligible girl, mutual attraction either occurs or does not occur based upon attributes that each values in the other. They may be looking for someone who possesses such abilities, qualities, or achievements as the same religion, a strong testimony, compatible values, a certain type of physical look, intelligence, humor, physical prowess, a good education, returned missionary status, good grooming, good manners, a good job or the potential to get one, compatible political views, and so on.

When they find someone with enough of these desired abilities, qualities, and achievements, they develop positive *feelings* toward the other and try to *show* their best behavior. Their behavior is usually as polite, kind, flattering, and flirtatious as they know how to be, which is known as courtship. There's often no better example of respect for one's mate than in the early development stage of the relationship. This is a stage that some authors call "falling in love," which is discussed in greater detail in chapter six.

True, eternal love cannot be reached unless both partners' feelings of respect for each other—based upon valued abilities, qualities, and achievements—are first developed. Then the respectful behavior that comes from these feelings quickly follows. It is problematic to attempt to start an intimate relationship before mutual feelings of respect occur.

A second stage in the development of love is sometimes called "disappointment," where our illusions of a perfect mate meet the reality of who they really are. Whether the relationship moves on to stage three ("acceptance") depends on being able to accept or learn to respect the new discoveries they make about their potential mate. With any luck, these discoveries are made long before marriage is even considered.

A few examples of reasons I've seen from my students breaking off engagements include the sudden discovery that their fiancé has an addiction to prescription drugs, alcohol, pornography, gambling, video gaming, or some other form. Or some live big lies, like they are not really enrolled in school or they don't really have a job or their sexual orientation is not as advertised. Others eventually figure out that men and women are different and decide they don't like those differences. They then try to remake their partner into something they do approve of, much to their partner's dismay. A loss of respect can quickly lead to a loss of love and commitment to a relationship.

Even if we do discover the real person before we marry, people change over time. The question is, can we tolerate and respect the direction our mate is choosing to grow? Can true, mature love continue to exist if, over time, we lose respect for our partner? I think the answer is no, as our feelings of respect for another directly affect the way we treat them and how we show our love for them. Maintaining respect is crucial for a successful marriage and takes a lot of honest communication and work.

Let's look at common mistakes couples make that cause a decrease in respectful feelings and actions over time. Afterward, we will look at things couples can do to maintain respect.

Things That Decrease Respect in Relationships

Undesirable Behavior

There are many behaviors that you or your partner might do that can be perceived as undesirable and diminish respect in each other's eyes.

The following is a partial list of behaviors I've heard from students in class discussions or in counseling sessions. The list is arranged somewhat from least disruptive in a relationship to the most serious:

- Snores
- Has gained too much weight and won't try to control it
- Doesn't call when coming home late
- Wears out his or her socks by wearing them around the house
- Drives too fast, too slow, tailgates, and so on
- Is habitually late for nearly everything
- Plays all-night online games with his or her brothers or buddies
- Spends too much time social networking on the Internet
- Spends too much time with his or her mother or father
- Won't do his or her share of the housework
- Is paranoid about keeping a clean house
- Won't preside (or won't allow him to preside)
- Won't diligently perform his or her Church callings
- Performs his or her Church calling with too much diligence and neglects the home calling
- Watches too many sports programs or daytime TV
- Is excessively critical and nagging about trivial things
- Is bossy and uncompromising
- Won't listen to complaints

- Would rather spend time with friends or relatives
- Is excessively materialistic and refuses to budget wisely
- Is too frugal and stingy with money
- Isn't interested enough in sexual intimacy
- Is too interested in sexual intimacy
- Wants to participate in sexual activities that are unacceptable to the other
- Lost their job or won't seriously try to get a job
- Insists that his wife work outside the home
- Is involved in pornography
- Is involved in inappropriate online relationships
- Becomes romantically and physically involved with another person
- Decides to no longer deny his or her same-sex attraction
- Loses his or her testimony and becomes only semi-active
- Decides to have his or her name removed from Church records
- Tries to force spouse and children to be inactive in the Church
- Wants to bring alcohol, tobacco, or illegal drugs into the home
- Abuses spouse or children (*abuse* is defined by the Church as "the physical, emotional, sexual, or spiritual mistreatment of others"[13])

These are all behaviors that can potentially disturb or destroy a relationship. Each person has to decide if these behaviors are just minor irritants that can be patiently overlooked and tolerated or are major violations of highly valued principles that cannot be endured under any circumstances. Or are they somewhere in between?

Questions we can ask ourselves include

- Will these behaviors affect me or our children's salvation?
- What battles are worth fighting and what behaviors are "deal breakers"?
- Do any of these irritants qualify as "nothing less serious than a prolonged and apparently irredeemable relationship which is destructive of a person's dignity as a human being"?[14]

There are other important questions that need to be answered also. Can you forgive someone who has crossed the line on unacceptable behavior but is willing to repent (see previous chapter)? Is the relationship irredeemable? Are you willing to pay the price necessary to work through differences of opinion on acceptable behavior? When, if ever, are you justified in not trying to help a loved one repent (see chapter nine on compassion)? Is their behavior physically dangerous to you or the rest of the family?

Few of these questions are easily answered. They require diligent prayer and soul-searching to make correct decisions. However, true love is something that seldom comes easily, and unless the divisive issues are successfully resolved, respect will be lost and eternal love never developed. All marriages eventually have problems with respect. The ones that survive and flourish are the ones that learn how to work through these differences. There many ways to resolve differences successfully. A brief summary of a few of my favorite techniques include:

- Before trying to solve problems, reassure each other there is dedicated commitment to the sacred covenants in the relationship. Stay positive; never lose sight of the ultimate goal and purpose of the marriage covenant and be determined to work through all obstacles and irritants until both partners are happy with the outcome.
- Patience, patience, and more patience in the process. Patience is closely related to maturity. Eternal love isn't possible without maturity.
- Communicate to understand in discussions before trying to solve the issue. Only one person has the floor at a time and the person without the floor should listen to understand. The speaker presents his or her viewpoint and then pauses so the listener can paraphrase back what was heard. When the speaker is certain the listener understands his or her points, then reverse roles. Only when complete understanding takes place can the discussions move on to seeking a solution. A good *Ensign* article on how to do this is by Elder Robert E. Wells, found in the January 1987 issue.

Unfortunately, there are many couples today who stay together and choose to reside in never-never land. Never-never land is a state where our inaction is never going to resolve the differences that diminish respect for each other and, as a result, we'll never find true love. This is unfortunate because all of us are capable of change if we can motivate ourselves enough to pay the price to do so.

President Hinckley's Counsel for Keeping Respect

President Gordon B. Hinckley and his wife gave advice on maintaining respect in marriage during an interview on their sixtieth wedding anniversary:

> "Develop and maintain respect for one another," he counseled. "You have to give and take in marriage. Another thing is a soft answer, keeping your voice down. Don't lose your temper. Speak quietly. There will be differences, but don't get stirred up over them. Just be quiet and calm and speak softly one to another."
>
> "Some people try to remake their spouse," said Sister Hinckley.
>
> *"Recognize your differences,"* said President Hinckley. "You will find that is a very wholesome and stimulating thing."
>
> "[Marriage] requires a very substantial measure of self-discipline. Marriage is not all romance. Marriage is work. Marriage is effort. You have to accommodate one another. You have to look after one another. Another thing is to do everything you can to develop the talents, the resources, the opportunities of your companion."[15]

President Hinckley gave similar counsel in a 1984 broadcast fireside: "Each of us is an individual. Each of us is different. There must be respect for those differences, and while it is important and necessary that both the husband and the wife strive to ameliorate those differences, there must be some recognition that they exist and that they are not necessarily undesirable. There must be respect one for another, not withstanding such differences. In fact, the differences may make the companionship more interesting."[16]

How Pride Kills Respect

Rather than trying to list all the potential ways bad behavior can blow up relationships, let's look at the detonators to the majority of these explosives and find ways to defuse them.

The origin of the majority of all serious relationship-destroying behaviors listed above comes from pride, in one form or another. Pride is the gateway sin that leads us to distort reality and fail to see the simple cause-and-effect consequences of our bad behaviors. Or, if we can see through our pride and accurately predict what will happen if we do something potentially harmful, pride causes us to not care about the injurious consequences, as long as we get our way.

Alma 45:24 explained the origins of this kind of pride: "But they grew proud, being lifted up in their hearts, because of their exceedingly great riches; therefore they grew rich in their own eyes, and would not give heed to their words, to walk uprightly before God."

Fame

The principle here is not necessarily the evils of wealth. We can substitute nearly any type of fame for wealth that leads to our being lifted up in our heart and growing famous in our own eyes. One result of seeing ourselves as famous is not giving heed to the words of others, and that is one of the greatest forms of disrespect we can show—especially to our eternal companion.

King Benjamin taught this principle at the beginning of his famous speech to the Nephites when he warned his people, "My brethren, all ye that have assembled yourselves together, you that can hear my words which I shall speak unto you this day; for I have not commanded you to come up hither to trifle with the words which I shall speak, but that you should hearken unto me" (Mosiah 2:9). Pride causes us to "trifle" with the words and feelings of others. Trifle means to treat something as trivial and undeserving of our time and attention. Trifling with someone's words and feelings nearly always guarantees the issue will remain unresolved, and we remain stuck in never-never land.

Entitlements

Unless carefully and consciously kept in check, the perception of fame naturally leads us to pride and sets off a cascading series of events. Unrepentant pride unsurprisingly leads to feelings of entitlement. Commercial advertising doesn't help in this area when we hear or read ads that proclaim, "You deserve a new car." "You deserve a vacation." "You deserve _____." What is the logic of these types of ads? Just what did any of us do that made us deserve these products, and how do they know we did it? They are not targeting our logic, nor are we thinking logically if we actually believe we deserve special perks in intimate relationships just because we have grown famous in our own eyes.

Competition and Disrespect

When perceived fame leads to pride and pride leads to irrational feelings of entitlement, feelings of entitlement lead to feelings of competition and disrespect. Pride causes us to disrespect anyone competitively seen as above us, and we look for ways to elevate ourselves above that person. President Benson taught that this includes enmity or hatred, even for God. If a proud person has no respect for God, then what chances do prophets, stake presidents, bishops, teachers, police, and parents have in expecting respect from them?

Pride also has no respect for those whom we competitively see beneath us in talent, intelligence, opportunities for education, social order, race, religion, gender, occupation, age, political persuasion, material possessions, and so on. Nephi saw the last days and the prideful nature of the Gentiles' behavior and commented on how cruel the proud are against those they see as beneath them:

> And the Gentiles are lifted up in the pride of their eyes, and have stumbled, because of the greatness of their stumbling block, that they have built up many churches [a church as used here can be any set of false ideas or beliefs that make us feel superior to our fellow man or lessen our need for God and His commandments]; nevertheless, they put down the power and miracles of God, and preach up unto themselves their own wisdom and their own learning, that they may get gain and *grind upon the face of the poor* (2 Nephi 26:20; emphasis added).

Nephi quoted Isaiah in calling those of our day *mean*: "And the *mean* man boweth not down, and the great man humbleth himself not, therefore, forgive him not" (2 Nephi 12:9; emphasis added). I have observed the proud in many marriage counseling sessions over the years and have seen meanness raise its ugly head many times. It's hard to reason with a mean man or woman because they lack the humility to listen for understanding. Proud, mean people don't want to understand their partner's views; they just want their way.

The proud often view everyone as a competitor in the game of life and love. To feel good about themselves and their behavior, the proud have to win every type of contest and put down their competitors. Disrespect is highly competitive by nature and can destroy nearly any relationship if allowed to creep in the back door. It is the feelings of competition and disrespect for others that ultimately lead us to trifle with their words and feelings, take advantage of others, and "grind upon the face of the poor."

Eventually, a proud person will bring their competitive and disrespectful spirit home to their partner also. Unchecked pride affects an intimate relationship in a variety of ways. Disrespecting those we love by refusing to compromise and change behaviors that bother each other will keep us in never-never land and far from an eternal relationship. Furthermore, depending on the seriousness of the behavior, stubborn pride can permanently end even committed eternal relationships.

Keeping Fame and Pride in Check

In order to not become "lifted up in the pride of [our] own eyes" and destroy our chances of finding and keeping true love, there are some basic things we can do. These basic tasks are like being asked to wash in the Jordan River seven times as Naaman was told to do in the Old Testament.[17] Naaman was at first wroth with Elisha because the task was too simple. Had he been asked to do "some great thing," he would have consented readily. However, isn't this the nature of pride? Pride insists on being above everything because we deserve special entitlements.

The first simple thing is to develop an attitude of gratitude for all we have. The proud are seldom (if ever) satisfied with what they have and are always seeking greater excess and fame. The Savior spoke of a proud rich man having to pull down his barns and build greater ones to hold all his surplus goods (Luke 12:16–21). In the end, his worldly goods were of little use.

Another simple thing to do in keeping unrighteous pride in check is following both the greatest commandments, found in Matthew 22:36–40. "Master, which is the great commandment in the law? Jesus said unto him, Thou shalt love the Lord thy God with all thy heart, and with all thy soul, and with all thy mind. This is the first and great commandment. And the second is like unto it, Thou shalt love thy neighbour as thyself. On these two commandments hang all the law and the prophets."

Pride teaches us to do just the opposite. One of the best examples in the scriptures is when Cain defiantly proclaimed, "Who is the Lord that I should know him?" (Moses 5:16). If we respect God and do not see His commandments as being beneath us, we will naturally follow the second great commandment to love our neighbors as ourselves.

This attitude of respect and equality for others alone will kill most prideful behaviors, because selfishness is its greatest manifestation. The Savior explained that all of God's law and the teachings of His prophets hang on our understanding and living these two simple but great commandments. There should be adequate motivation to overcome all our relationship-destroying behaviors if we sincerely ask ourselves, "How would I feel if that were being done to me?" The Savior teaches us to ask this question; pride teaches us to selfishly forget it.

We will examine President Benson's thoughts on pride in greater detail and give more specific suggestions for keeping pride in check in later chapters.

Scriptural Admonitions to Show Respect to One Another

The following scriptures and quotation from President Gordon B. Hinckley should remind us of the importance of treating others—especially our eternal mate—with the respect they deserve as children of God:

- "Let no corrupt communication proceed out of your mouth, but that which is good to the use of edifying, that it may minister grace unto the hearers. And grieve not the holy Spirit of God, whereby ye are sealed unto the day of redemption. Let all bitterness, and wrath, and anger, and clamour, and evil speaking, be put away from you, with all malice: And be ye kind one to another, tenderhearted, forgiving one another, even as God for Christ's sake hath forgiven you" (Ephesians 4:29–32).
- "So ought men to love their wives as their own bodies. He that loveth his wife loveth himself. For no man ever yet hated his own flesh; but nourisheth and cherisheth it, even as the Lord the church: For we are members of his body, of his flesh, and of his bones. For this cause shall a man leave his father and mother, and shall be joined unto his wife, and they two shall

be one flesh. This is a great mystery: but I speak concerning Christ and the church. Nevertheless let every one of you in particular so love his wife even as himself; and the wife see that she reverence her husband" (Ephesians 5:28–33).

- "For behold, there is a wo pronounced upon him who listeth to obey that spirit [the spirit of contention]" (Mosiah 2:32–33).
- "And ye will not have a mind to injure one another, but to live peaceably, and to render to every man according to that which is his due" (Mosiah 4:12–13).
- "And he commanded them that there should be no contention one with another, but that they should look forward with one eye, having one faith and one baptism, having their hearts knit together in unity and in love one towards another" (Mosiah 18:21).
- "For our words will condemn us, yea, all our works will condemn us; we shall not be found spotless; and our thoughts will also condemn us; and in this awful state we shall not dare to look up to our God; and we would fain be glad if we could command the rocks and the mountains to fall upon us to hide us from his presence" (Alma 12:14).

President Gordon B. Hinckley: "There are so many in our day who are unwilling to forgive and forget. Children cry and wives weep because fathers and husbands continue to bring up little shortcomings that are really of no importance. And there also are many women who would make a mountain out of every little offending molehill of word or deed."[18]

Summary

Early in the chapter, we reviewed Abraham Maslow's hierarchy of needs. Maslow wrote that our "lower esteem" needs are usually determined by how others perceive us, based upon our accomplishments. He also wrote that our "higher esteem" are based on how we feel about ourselves. Low self-esteem in either area can wreck intimate relationships because the feelings we have about ourselves usually determine the way we feel about others. "If we don't love ourselves, it's impossible to show much love for anybody else—especially our spouse."[19]

All five of the dictionary definitions of respect contained the words *feel* and *show*. When we respect someone, it's because we have developed feelings of approval based upon their combination of abilities, qualities or achievements. We then naturally show respect for them by treating them in polite, kind ways. Respect means we first have positive *feelings* toward someone, and then *show* our respect through our actions.

There are many factors that cause respect to be lost in intimate relationships. I presented a list of typical irritants in marriage, ranging from such minor things as snoring and failing to call home when running late to atomic bombs like adultery, apostasy, and abuse. I suggested that pride is a common element in nearly all of these behaviors and recommended three general principles for keeping pride and these types of relationship-destroying behaviors in check: develop an attitude of gratitude for all you have, follow the greatest of all commandments to love God, and follow the second great commandment to love our neighbors as ourselves.

Principle of Respect Self-Evaluation Questions

- Concerning Maslow's definition of "lower esteem," how do you feel about yourself?
  - A. I've accomplished enough at this point in my life to feel I'm on the right path and making good progress toward my divine destiny. I feel I have much to offer an eternal mate.
  - B. At times, I feel I get off the path to my divine destiny and need to make a few course corrections.

- Concerning Maslow's definition of "higher esteem," how do you feel about yourself?
  - A. I have adequate feelings of self-respect, confidence, achievement, competence, independence, and freedom to be happy in an intimate relationship.
  - B. There are times when I feel I have little of worth to offer someone in a marriage relationship.

- Do you engage in any behaviors that have the potential to diminish respect for you in the eyes of your companion or a potential companion?
  - A. No
  - B. Yes

- Can you start eliminating unrighteous pride from your life and relationships?
  A. No
  B. Yes

Chapter 6: Understanding True Love

![banner]

Successful marriages and families are established and maintained by understanding the elements and composition of true love.

This chapter focuses on defining what mature love is and isn't and how that knowledge can keep us from making mistakes in our love lives. Chapter seven will discuss thirteen specific actions we can do or avoid doing to help us find a love that can last for all eternity.

Understanding the Principle of Love in Intimate Relationships

Defining love is quite a challenge as it is so multifaceted. It can be applied to courtship and marriage situations in almost infinite ways. Henry Fink theorized in 1887 that "love is such a tissue of paradoxes, and exists in such an endless variety of forms and shades that you may say almost anything about it that you please, and it is likely to be correct."[20]

Sages, poets, and philosophers have defined love many different ways over the centuries. One of the oldest definitions comes from the ancient Greeks. They divided love into three elements. First, *eros*, or the erotic physical or sexual side of love; second, *agape*, or the altruistic and non-demanding part of love (*agape* also often means a divine, unconditional, self-sacrificing, active, volitional, and thoughtful form of love); and third is *philos*, or the type of love that is found in deep friendships.

Paul Tillich (August 20, 1886–October 22, 1965), one of the most influential Protestant theologians of the twentieth century, felt the highest form of love between a man and a woman is a combination of *eros* and *agape*: "No love is real without a unity of *eros* and *agape*. *Agape* without *eros* is obedience to moral law, without warmth, without longing, without reunion. *Eros* without *agape* is a chaotic desire, denying the validity of the claim of the other one to be acknowledged as an independent self, able to love and to be loved."[21]

President Gordon B. Hinckley provided the definition that best fits the action principles of love used later in this chapter. Unlike Tillich, President Hinckley seemed to downplay the over-importance of romance, or *eros*, in our everyday interactions. But like Tillich, he appeared to see love as practical actions, a verb rather than a noun with more of the attributes of *agape* and *philos* than *eros*.

President Hinckley spoke of the type of love that leads to a true and lasting happiness in marriage, which stems from loving actions that consistently take place on an everyday basis. These actions should not take place only on Valentine's Day, birthdays, or anniversaries, or when one partner's sexual needs are piqued: "I am satisfied that happiness in marriage is not so much a matter of romance as it is an anxious concern for the comfort and well-being of one's companion. Any man who will make his wife's comfort his first concern will stay in love with her throughout their lives and through the eternity yet to come."[22]

Love is many things to many people, but for the purposes of this chapter, love is first and foremost an "anxious concern for the comfort and well-being" of our eternal mate or eternal mate-to-be. I don't discount the importance of *eros* in love; it is certainly a vital part of the equation. I completely agree with Tillich that "*agape* without *eros* is obedience to moral law, without warmth, without longing, without reunion." I've seen relationships like this and they are best described as incomplete and unsatisfying. However, I don't believe the world needs more advice about, attention to, or methods of *eros*. The information age, complete with electronic media and the written word, seems fixated on *eros* and provides a raging river of information that we are told to drink daily. It shouldn't take an entire lake of water to satisfy our thirst.

What I believe is in short supply is the knowledge of how to demonstrate love in intimate relationships in altruistic, non-demanding, godlike, unconditional, self-sacrificing, everyday thoughtful forms of *agape* that lead us to becoming *philos* (best friends) as well as *eros* (lovers). I also believe the best way to improve *eros* romantic relationship is to concentrate first on the other two. Great *eros* love naturally follows successful *agape* and *philos* loving actions. An easy way to remember this is with the acronym APE: First, A (*agape*), then P (*philos*), and after those E (*eros*) naturally follows.

The following chapter attempts to demonstrate a variety of ways to do this. First, however, let's look at elements of and counterfeits of true, mature love.

Practical Applications of Love Knowledge

In chapter one, we discussed a companion-selection paradigm using the revealed truths of Alma 32 and the development of faith as an outline for finding and keeping true love. Alma 32 is a powerful model to use in trying to develop true love, but there is more to learn.

Application 1: Understanding Counterfeit Love Helps Us to Not Be Deceived about True Love

Many students over the years talked to me about their mistakes in this area and the dire consequences from these adventures. Erich Fromm wrote in 1956, "Desire can be stimulated by the anxiety of aloneness, by the wish to conquer or be conquered, by vanity, by the wish to hurt or even to destroy, as much as it can be stimulated by love."[23]

I recall a beautiful young lady years ago who managed to get herself into a relationship that violated all four of Fromm's warnings about mistaken love (fear of loneliness, wish to conquer, vanity, and wish to hurt or destroy). After attending a large evening institute dating and courtship class for several weeks with her boyfriend, she came to see me. She had on sunglasses, and when she took them off she revealed a black eye. She told me her boyfriend had struck her. She told me of the sexual, emotional, and physical abuse in their dating relationship.

As a rule in counseling settings, I refrain from specific advice on what to do and instead point out probable consequences and what I believe to be correct principles of conduct. In this case, I blurted out, "Why are you still with this guy? Do you need help placing a restraining order on him to keep his distance from you?" I assured her she would have no problem finding a better man at the institute.

Her answer surprised me at the time, but I've heard it repeated so often now that I'm not anymore. She said she was in *love* with him and was more afraid of being *alone* than being hurt.

She wasn't in college at the time and had few social opportunities at work or otherwise. This young man came from a wealthy family; she came from a financially disadvantaged setting. He was good-looking, popular, and had introduced her to a whole set of friends and expanded social circles. He had convinced her he was the best thing that had ever happened to her and she now owed him whatever he wanted from her. What he wanted from her was to be seen with her so as to feed his *vanity*, to *conquer* her, and then *destroy* her, apparently so no one else could have her. He hit her because she caught him with another woman, and he expected her to just accept it and wait for him to call for her again when it pleased him.

Other female students have also told me it is much harder than I realize to get out of this kind of a relationship. It bothered me greatly that she chose to stay with him and continued facing the abuse he was giving her.

However, a few weeks later, something wonderful happened. She came to class alone as her boyfriend had some other things to do. Before the night was over, three sharp returned missionaries had asked her for her phone number and permission to call. Suddenly, the light came on and she realized she had other social options and deserved better than what her soon-to-be-ex was giving her.

When she told him that they were through, he was upset at the prospect of losing his *conquest* and source of *vanity* and *power*. Fortunately, she stood her ground and, with the help of her older brothers and the police, he finally decided to leave her alone. With additional help of her bishop, she was able to see things from an eternal perspective and get her life back together.

Premarital Sex and Counterfeit Love

Eric Fromm (March 1900–March 1980) in his international bestseller *The Art of Loving* also helps us understand why sex before marriage is so often confused with true love:

> It seems that sexual desire can easily blend with and be stimulated by any strong emotion, of which love is only one. Because sexual desire is in the minds of most people coupled with the idea of love, they are easily misled to conclude that they love each other when they want each other physically. . . . [But] if [this] desire . . . is not stimulated by real love, it . . . leaves strangers as far apart as they were before—sometimes it makes them ashamed of each other, or even makes them hate each other, because when the illusion has gone, they feel their estrangement even more markedly than before.[24]

Many Church leaders have warned members of the dangers of confusing the feelings associated with sexual intimacy before marriage with true love. Elder Spencer W. Kimball explained how sexual relations before marriage could actually destroy love instead of being the pathway to true love: "At the hour of sin, pure love is pushed out of one door while lust sneaks in the other. Affection has then been replaced with desire of the flesh and uncontrolled passion. Accepted has been the doctrine which the devil is so eager to establish, that illicit sex relations are justified."[25]

Elder Boyd K. Packer further stated how common this deception is in our world today:

> The greatest deception foisted upon the human race in our day is that overemphasis of physical gratification as it is related to romantic love. It is merely a repetition of the same delusion that has been impressed on every generation in ages past. When we learn that physical gratification is only incident to, and not the compelling force of love itself, we have made a supreme discovery. If only physical gratification should interest you, you need not be selective at all. This power is possessed by almost everyone. Alone, without attendant love, this relationship becomes nothing—indeed, less and worse than nothing.[26]

Studies done at BYU and published in *Journal of Family Psychology* in February 2011 show the wisdom of the prophets' warnings about love and premarital relations:

The BYU researchers found that couples that waited until marriage before having sex reported 22 percent higher relational stability, 20 percent higher relational satisfaction, 15 percent better sexual quality, and 12 percent better communication.

Those benefits were cut in half for couples who waited a significant amount of time into the relationship, yet still had sex before marriage.[27]

Knowledge is power, and knowledge of how not to ruin love before it gets a chance to get started is helpful.

Application 2: Understanding the Elements of True Love Can Determine if a Dating Relationship Should Be an Eternal One

In addition to and in support of revealed plan of salvation truths about love, in this section we also look at a few social science theories about true love and how it is formed. We will see that all of these classic social science theories suggest love has numerous parts and various stages of development.

Goldstein's Three Stages of Love

In their 1977 bestseller *The Dance-Away Lover*, Daniel Goldstein and colleagues[28] theorized that love evolves in three fairly predictable stages. Stage one is "falling in love." It consists of lots of excitement, emotional highs, good feelings both about self and your partner, putting your best foot forward, and being just short of blind to the shortcomings of your beloved. This is a fleeting stage and all it really tells is that two people are strongly attracted to each other. It isn't yet true love, but it's an exciting start.

Stage two is "disappointment." Sooner or later, conflicts arise as your partner's behavior fails to match your ideal expectations of them and vice versa. The realities of the situation set in and must now be faced. Can you accept each other's faults or will you cling to the idealized image of the perfect mate and go look somewhere else? The lesson learned from understanding these somewhat normal phenomena is that just because disappointments happen does not mean that you're not in love or that the relationship must end. Love and marriage are like parenting in that it isn't a merry-go-round; it's much more like a rollercoaster with a lot of ups and downs.

Stage three is "acceptance." If you and your partner can survive stage two and learn to work through your differences, then trust can replace disappointment and disillusionment, and you can move on to a deep shared intimacy based upon actual knowledge of each other rather than based on the fantasies of stage one.

Fromm's Six Foundational Elements of Mature Love

Again from Eric Fromm's classic book *The Art of Loving*, Fromm believes that mature love includes attachment plus sexual response (*eros*). In other words, the first two steps of his six-part formula are a deep desire to be with one another and a sexual attraction toward one another. Without these two foundation stones, young relationships wither and die rather quickly.

Elder Bruce R. McConkie put it this way: "The right person is someone for whom the natural and wholesome and normal affection that should exist does exist. It is the person who is living so that he or she can go to the temple of God and make the covenants that we there make."[29]

Having a "natural and wholesome and normal affection" for someone doesn't mean that we are destined to act uncontrollably on our sexual instincts. It means there should be something stirred inside us when we see each other. In addition to attachment and *eros*, Fromm says there are four other basic elements necessary to true, mature love: care, responsibility, respect, and knowledge. These four elements are close to the meaning of *agape* and what President Hinckley and others have said are the mainstay of love that can last for eternity.

Care means we are mature enough to care about the needs of someone else, even at the expense of our own wishes. It means we are willing to sacrifice our own needs and wants for the good of the relationship. Mature love is not possible without this foundation stone in place. Unfortunately, the modern-day young adult lifestyle and values don't naturally lead our young men and women in this direction.

Responsibility is the moral responsibility that each person has to the marriage and the resulting family unit. With responsibility comes a moral obligation to such things as commitment, sexual exclusivity, fidelity, and fulfilling our gender roles as defined in the plan of salvation. Again, modern society doesn't seem to steer youth in this direction. Respect is so important that this book has an entire chapter (five) devoted to it.

Knowledge is the intimate familiarity we gain as we pay attention to details and learn all we can about each other. What are your partner's greatest fears? What can you best do to help him or her? When do you back off and when do you strongly step forward to the rescue? What are his or her favorite foods, books, movies, colors, and hobbies? What makes him or her happy?

Eternal mates and potential eternal mates don't come with instruction manuals. If we ever hope to reach the level of couple unity necessary for exaltation, we need to learn all we can, whenever we can, about our partner. This necessity means we never neglect, ignore, or reprioritize them.

Again, sadly, the modern materialistic, "what's in it for me" age we live in does not value investigating others enough to see how we can better love them. Today's environment seems to tell us in daily advertising and entertainment, "Get all you can from others. Discover their weaknesses and learn to exploit these to achieve your own ambitions."

The Savior summed up our times concisely when prophesying about the last days in Matthew 24:12: "And because iniquity shall abound, the love of many shall wax cold." Our Lord repeated this appraisal of our times to Joseph Smith in Doctrine and Covenants 45:27: "And the love of men shall wax cold, and iniquity shall abound."

Iniquity and love cannot coexist. Iniquity thinks exclusively of itself, whereas love focuses on the needs of others. Iniquity loves things and uses people, whereas true love reverses that order. Iniquity is ruled by the natural man's lusts of the flesh, but true love has learned this important lesson: "Also see that ye bridle all your passions, that ye may be filled with love" (Alma 38:12).

The contrast between pure love by living a righteous life versus living a life of self-centered wickedness is spoken of many times in the scriptures:

- "Many sorrows shall be to the wicked: but he that trusteth in the Lord, mercy shall compass him about" (Psalm 32:10).
- "There is no peace, saith my God, to the wicked" (Isaiah 57:21).

- "For ye have sought all the days of your lives for that which ye could not obtain; and ye have sought for happiness in doing iniquity, which thing is contrary to the nature of that righteousness which is in our great and Eternal Head" (Helaman 13:38).
- "Do not suppose, because it has been spoken concerning restoration, that ye shall be restored from sin to happiness. Behold, I say unto you, wickedness never was happiness" (Alma 41:10).

There were logical reasons for these Old Testament and Book of Mormon prophets to proclaim that wickedness never was happiness. Whichever path we choose to pursue—one of wickedness and aloneness or one of righteousness and true love—taking that path will cause the other to fade.

Couples wise enough to overcome this natural man world and who learn to share all six basic elements become what Fromm called "pair-bonded" in a reciprocal relationship. The result of being pair-bonded is to move toward feelings of unity, completeness (reaching our divine destiny), selflessness, and happiness, which is the true object and design of our existence.

Sternberg's Three Elements of Love

Robert Sternberg, an American psychologist and psychometrician, provost at Oklahoma State University, and former president of the American Psychological Association, presented a simple model that suggested only three main elements within love: intimacy, passion, and commitment.[30] *Intimacy* (a form of *agape*) is detailed knowledge of our mate learned over time by paying attention and caring enough to remember it. *Passion* (a form of *eros*) is caring enough to not let the fire burn out. *Commitment* (another form of *agape*) means showing loyalty to something or someone, in this case your mate.

Sternberg devised seven different names for types of love created by possessing one, two, or all three elements:

- *Empty love*: Commitment without intimacy and passion
- *Liking*: Intimacy without passion or commitment
- *Infatuated love*: Passion without intimacy or commitment
- *Romantic love*: Intimacy and passion without commitment
- *Companionate love*: Intimacy and commitment without passion

- *Fatuous love*: Passion and commitment without intimacy
- *Consummate love*: A perfectly balanced combination of all three elements

The Similarity Principle

Our last definition of true love has its roots in the similarity principle, which says that "the more alike two people are in intimate relationships, the greater the probability that the relationship will succeed."[31]

As the following figure shows, not all areas of compatibility are equal, nor is the amount of compatibility in each area.

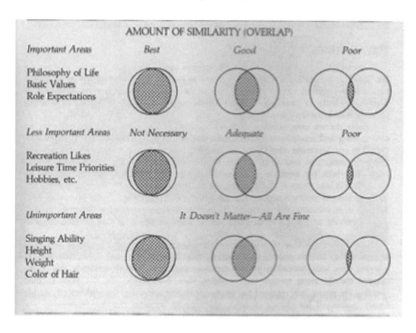

As a doctoral student at Brigham Young University, I coauthored a relationship assessment tool in 1979 that was eventually called the *Relate*. It has evolved and improved greatly over the years and is currently administered by the Relate Institute at the university.

The *Relate* (in 2015) consists of a questionnaire with 276 question found to be predictive of later marital quality. When couples take the questionnaire, they receive an eleven-page report with twelve graphs and charts showing how they rate various aspects of their relationship compared to their partner's views. The *Relate* can be helpful to couples looking to discover potential areas of disagreement to work on before they decide to marry.

Once, I listened to a student tell me how surprised he was to learn *after his marriage* that his wife didn't want children. He had just assumed she wanted six, just like he did. The marriage ended in divorce, as this was an important value to each of them and neither was willing to compromise in this area. This couple and others like them would have benefited from taking the *Relate* before they became engaged. You can find the *Relate* online by searching on BYU Relate Institute.

Inquire Well

With any luck, this review of a few of the classical definitions of love may be helpful to those wondering if the feelings they have for someone are actually love and if that love has the ability to stand the test of time. Elder Dallin H. Oaks counseled in general conference in 2007: "I speak briefly to those contemplating marriage. The best way to avoid divorce from an unfaithful, abusive, or unsupportive spouse is to avoid marriage to such a person. If you wish to marry well, inquire well."[32]

I have included a questionnaire for mature love at the end of chapter seven that may help those not yet married to inquire well before taking the leap. For those already married, it can help you find neglected areas where mature love can be strengthened.

Summary

Sages, poets, and philosophers have defined love in many different ways. We looked at three different forms given to us from the Greeks: *eros*, sexual or physical; *agape*, altruistic, non-demanding, unconditional, self-sacrificing, active, volitional, thoughtful; and *philos*, the type of love that is found in deep friendships. President Gordon B. Hinckley emphasized that true love is based more upon an "anxious concern for the comfort and well-being" of your partner than anything else.

I listed a few counterfeits of true love so that they will not deceive you. These include the anxiety of aloneness, the wish to conquer or be conquered, vanity, a wish to hurt or even destroy someone, and basic sexual desires.

We examined three different approaches showing elements or stages of true love so as to help determine if a dating relationship should progress into an eternal marriage or not. David Goldstein and colleagues theorized that love evolves in three often-predictable stages: falling in love, disappointment, and acceptance.

Eric Fromm gave us six foundational elements of mature love: attachment, sexual response, caring, responsibility, respect, and knowledge. Robert Sternberg presented a simpler model by suggesting only three main elements within love: intimacy, passion, and commitment.

Finally, we reviewed the similarity principle that says "the more alike two people are in intimate relationships, the greater the probability that the relationship will succeed."

Chapter 7: Applying True Love Principles-Part 1

Successful marriages and families are established and maintained by understanding and correctly applying true principles of love.

The most important knowledge about love is how to apply it to our everyday lives. President Hinckley counseled that we keep true love alive with an "anxious concern for the comfort and well-being of one's companion." How exactly do we do this? How do we better demonstrate love in non-demanding, self-sacrificing, everyday actions that are appreciated by those we love and ultimately bring us to greater unity? This chapter looks at ways to do that.

Moroni's Definition of Perfect Love

Again, we look to the past for wisdom. True principles are always true, in all cultures and throughout all time. This definition of love is from the writings of Moroni, though the Apostle Paul gives the same list in 1 Corinthians 13. (Any of God's counsel repeated in separate volumes of scripture to different peoples tells us the message is especially important.)

Moroni calls mature love "charity," or "the pure love of Christ" (Moroni 7:47), or an "everlasting" and "perfect love" (Moroni 8:17). He says this perfect love is so important that without learning it before we die, we are basically "nothing" and thus have failed the test of our mortal existence (Moroni 7:44, 46). Moroni's perfect love consists of thirteen things we need to do or not do.

Before examining the list, we should look at the cost for obtaining perfect love. This pearl of great price is available to all people; however, all seekers must be willing to climb to the top of a steep and difficult mountain to gain the greatest of all prizes: perfect and everlasting love and the happiness that accompanies it.

In Moroni 7:26, Moroni tells us that love is something we must ask God for as we cannot earn or purchase it totally on our own. This implies that charity is a gift of the Spirit to be diligently sought after and hoped for: "Whatsoever thing ye shall ask the Father in my name, which is good, in faith believing that ye shall receive, behold, it shall be done unto you."

Further, after presenting the list, Moroni says again that we must ask for it, but he adds an important additional requirement: "Wherefore, my beloved brethren, pray unto the Father with all the energy of heart, that ye may be filled with this love, which he hath bestowed upon all who *are true followers* of his Son, Jesus Christ; that ye may become the sons of God; that when he shall appear we shall be like him, for we shall see him as he is; that we may have this hope; that we may be purified even as he is pure" (Moroni 7:48; emphasis added).

Here, we learn that charity or perfect love is a gift that is "bestowed" upon those who are "true followers" of Christ. What is a true follower? One who loves God by keeping his commandments. After all, "If ye love me, keep my commandments" (John 14:15). Perfect love is too hard for any of us to learn on our own. To become one with another human being is beyond our natural capacities. To achieve such perfect love, God must bestow it upon us. It is a gift of the Spirit that comes to us by grace after we do all we can to earn it.

Moroni's Thirteen Elements of Perfect Love

Moroni 7:45 presents the list: "And charity suffereth long, and is kind, and envieth not, and is not puffed up, seeketh not her own, is not easily provoked, thinketh no evil, and rejoiceth not in iniquity but rejoiceth in the truth, beareth all things, believeth all things, hopeth all things, endureth all things."

This list consists of eight Christlike attributes we strive to emulate and five natural man behaviors we work to avoid. It's similar to a marriage counseling session where the therapist asks couples to make a list of behaviors they like their partner to do and another list of actions that really bother them. The goal is to do more of the "I like" list and less of the "it bothers me" list and become more consistent at both over time.

This chapter examines the eight positive attributes we should try to emulate. In order to do this, I've rearranged the order of Moroni's list to separate out the things we try to do more consistently from the things we try to avoid. I've also categorized several of the similar attributes under one general heading. We start with the general topic of patience.

Four of the thirteen attributes deal with patience in one form or another. Why? It is because patience is one of the most important aspects of mature true love? Could it be one of the hardest traits to master? I've grouped these four slightly different forms of patience together and will examine them all together.

Suffereth Long, Beareth All Things, Endureth All Things, Is Not Easily Provoked

Suffering long, bearing all things, enduring all things, and not being easily provoked are, among other things, the capacity to endure trouble, opposition, or anguish without becoming angry (easily provoked), frustrated, or overly anxious. If we can do this consistently over time, then even when we are tired or sick or just plain worn down, we have begun to learn to endure all things.

I say "begun to learn" the meaning of patience and enduring all things because, when compared to what Jesus Christ did for us, there is nothing we can endure that comes even remotely close to what He sacrificed for mankind. The epitome of patience—in being able to suffer long, bear all things, and endure all things without being provoked—comes from Nephi's description of our Savior's (at the time) future rejection by the wicked world: "And the world, because of their iniquity, shall judge him to be a thing of naught; wherefore they scourge him, and he suffereth it; and they smite him, and he suffereth it. Yea, they spit upon him, and he suffereth it, because of his loving kindness and his long suffering towards the children of men" (1 Nephi 19:9).

How many of us (and for how long) could endure being judged "a thing of naught"? The prisons today are full of men who murdered a fellow human being simply because they "dissed" them in some insignificant way. Not all of us react that violently, but few of us can take being disrespected by others for long. It hurts even more when disrespect comes from our eternal mate.

How many times could we be smitten physically before we became angry and retaliated in kind? To turn the other cheek requires great patience and maturity. Who could stand by and be spit upon and simply suffer it? This happened to me once, and it took every ounce of patience I possessed not to retaliate. It was in San Francisco in 1972 when I came back from Vietnam. As I walked out of the gate at the airport terminal, I was in military uniform when a group of hippie women insulted me. I don't think I could have restrained myself if they had been men. Their disrespect was not only to me but also to the great country I voluntarily served and was protecting for them. When I think about the incident all these years later, I still find myself not suffering it as the Savior would have me do.

Looking at patience from an eternal perspective, patience is necessary for our salvation. To be saved, we have to endure in righteousness to the end. Making and keeping covenants creates the commitment necessary for us to endure and put all our weaknesses under our feet.

Sometimes patience is the ability to accept God's will and timing in answers to earnest prayer. Suffering long is holding up under pressure and being able to face adversity calmly with hope and faith. Patience requires great faith and trust in the Lord's boundless love and wisdom.

I had a friend years ago whose young child contracted cancer. He and his family fasted and prayed for a miracle, and the cancer went into remission. They were ecstatic. Then the next year, it came back with a vengeance.

This time the entire ward fasted and prayed for the child, and again the cancer subsided. But eighteen months later, it came back, and again they prayed it away. For a fourth time it returned and as my friend prayed for understanding, he was given this impression: "Three times

I've tried to take your son back . . . it's time to let him go." The family finally understood and, though they suffered long yet, they bore it well.

Is Not Easily Provoked

"Bearing all things" and not being "easily provoked" also require patience (though in less dramatic, everyday experiences), especially with the companions we spend so much time with. "Long suffering" requires tolerance with all people, including ourselves, as we work to overcome faults and weaknesses.

Great patience is important at each stage of a relationship. In the courtship stage, sooner or later we all realize our partner is not perfect. Can we suffer through this disappointment and the demise of our imagined perfect mate and learn to accept, appreciate, and love our real mate for who they really are? Can we tolerate the imperfections found in another? The New Testament teaches us to not judge another's faults when we ourselves are found wanting. This counsel also works for marriages and relationships.

Many struggle, for instance, in early marriage with the discovery that their sexual needs are not always in perfect harmony and timing with their partner's. Can we suffer through these frustrations patiently in hopes of greater understanding?

When children arrive, many wonder what happened to the unique friendship and lover stage of courtship and early marriage that now must be shared with a new family. Can we be patient when our partner pays increasing amounts of attention to the children? Does our lack of patience demand the same amount of attention we used to get before the arrival of children?

When the children leave home and the nest is again empty, can we suffer through the feelings of emptiness and loss of purpose that many feel? Can we empathize with our partner's suffering, even if we (usually men) may not feel the same intensity? Can we accept the changing seasons of our lives with dignity, grace, and endurance?

Can we suffer through our partner's natural changes in life? What are we going to do when menopause collides head-on with midlife crises? I've seen it get ugly. Can we adapt without being "easily provoked"? Can we suffer the frustrations of our partner losing interest in intimacy before we do as we age?

Can we endure the hardships of illnesses or accidents with our eternal mate and cheerfully do our duty to the best of our ability? Can we bear it if our partner gains weight, goes prematurely gray, needs a new hip, or blows out a knee?

If you're young and fit and reading this, beware. Time marches on and our bodies wear out. Your love had better be based on far more than physical attraction and *eros* feelings. Yes, bearing all things is part of the partnership and the price that must be paid if we expect to create a true and eternal love and thereby reach our divine destiny one day.

Is it possible to learn the meaning of patience without being married? There are undoubtedly many circumstances in life that can teach us to bear all things besides marriage, but I suspect there are certain aspects of patience that only a long-term marriage can teach us.

For myself, I seem to have always been able to deal with large problems and intense situations in a rational and calm manner. I've been shot at in Vietnam and didn't panic. I've been through potentially horrific near misses in traffic on the freeways and kept my composure. In athletic contests, the right thing to do seemed to come to me instinctively in intense situations.

However, it is often the little things in family life where I have sometimes failed to bear all things with composure and patience. Why do we sometimes lose our tempers over seemingly small and insignificant (in the eternal scheme of things) incidents? Why can't we all just get along? Sometimes something as simple as the failure to immediately pick something up off the floor that we drop or the way we do the dishes creates the same amount of drama as eternally important issues in marriage such as Church attendance or being totally faithful.

"Bearing all things" might mean learning to patiently and carefully choose those things worth fighting for and being able to ignore the rest, even though at the time we might think we are going to explode from frustration. Take a deep breath, count to ten, go to your happy place. Just let it go. Refuse to be the one who is always taking offense at comments or actions. Make sure each event is worth the energy and effort it takes to work through it. Nagging, contention, and power struggles can be reduced considerably if we set our minds to it.

Is Kind

Though we could argue that kindness can be grouped with patience as it often takes patience to be kind, I've given it its own place, as did Paul and Moroni.

Kindness is known as a virtue. In Christian theology, charity, or love (*agape*), means an unlimited loving-kindness toward all others.

Just how hard is it to be kind? How hard should it be? Is it the pace and pressures of modern living we bring into the home that inadvertently cause us to be unkind to the people we love the most? Should our familiarity and level of comfort with each other allow us to be less than civil in marriage? What kind of an example do unkind parents set for their children?

King Benjamin warned us about setting a proper example in this area for our children:

> And ye will not have a mind to injure one another, but to live peaceably, and to render to every man according to that which is his due. And ye will not suffer your children that they go hungry, or naked; neither will ye suffer that they transgress the laws of God, and fight and quarrel one with another, and serve the devil, who is the master of sin, or who is the evil spirit which hath been spoken of by our fathers, he being an enemy to all righteousness (Mosiah 4:13–14).

Would a couple that prays with each other and for each other every day seldom, if ever, be unkind to each other? Would a couple who attends the temple regularly be less likely to act unkindly toward one other, or to any others?

Kindness includes consistently treating each other in a civil manner. The word *civility* is most often defined as behavior between persons and groups that conforms to a social mode (that is, in accordance with the civil society). Concerning civility, President Hinckley once said, "But civility also appears to be fading much closer to home. Civility covers a host of matters in the relationships among human beings. Its presence is described in such terms as 'good manners' and 'good breeding.' But everywhere about us we see the opposite."[33]

To President Hinckley, there is a social mode or a set of behavioral expectations that Latter-day Saints should be willing to conform to in the way we treat each other. Marriage does not negate that expectation for the way we act in the home when no outsiders are watching us. Truly, if we hope to follow President Hinckley's admonition to have "an anxious concern for the comfort and well-being of one's companion," we need to strive to be kind to each other.

Believeth All Things, Hopeth All Things

These true love characteristics mean we see our marriage with optimism, trust, and determination rather than with pessimism, distrust, and irresolution.

Optimism is a disposition or tendency to look on the more favorable side of events or conditions and to expect the most favorable outcome. It is the belief that good ultimately overcomes evil in the fallen world we now inhabit. In the words of Nephi, it is "having a perfect brightness of hope, and a love of God and of all men" (2 Nephi 31:20).

To believe all things means we have a positive mind-set and attitude that eventually defines our personality and the way we treat people. We can train our minds to view things either optimistically or pessimistically. We can have hope and belief in the face of difficult challenges, or we can easily give up in despair. The choice is always ours.

In 2009, I taught an institute of religion class for LDS football players of the University of Utah. After an incredible comeback against an undefeated TCU team, the players told me the following story: Late in the fourth quarter and behind 13–6, Utah had only been able to score two field goals and was unable to move the ball with any consistency against the TCU defense. With less than two minutes to go, TCU lined up for an easy field goal that would put the game out of reach. Many Utah fans got up and left the stadium. TCU missed the field goal and Utah had the ball eighty yards away from taking the lead. Many fans continued to leave the stadium, having given up on their team.

In the huddle before the first play of the final drive, Utah's quarterback, Brian Johnson, saw the fans leaving and told his teammates. "Too bad they're leaving. They're going to miss a great winning touchdown drive." His teammates nodded in agreement and believed him. He then directed his teammates to a perfectly executed drive that resulted in the winning touchdown. Utah went on to deliver an undefeated 12–0 regular season and an invitation to the Sugar Bowl.

Brian showed that same belief and hope in the Sugar Bowl. Utah played against an outstanding Alabama team, who the newspapers said was so much better than Utah that there was no player on the Utah team good enough for them to want to recruit. The TV announcers even predicted a blowout win for Alabama because Utah was so outmatched. At the end of the first quarter, the score was Utah-28, Alabama-0, and there was no way to stop Utah's momentum. An attitude of hope and belief is everything in sports, life, and love.

Don't Let Fear Make You Leave the Stadium or the Home Too Early

It is truly a sad thing to see couples married long enough that they lose the novelty of the new relationship and their initial optimistic outlook toward their eternal mate. In the early years of their marriage, their newfound soul mate could do no wrong. However, many couples today decide to leave the stadium at the first sign of disappointment or trouble.

Believing all things means to give your partner the benefit of the doubt. It is closely related to the seventh attribute of charity: hoping all things. It keeps you fully committed when the hard times come, which they will.

Our class motto for the fifty-five LDS players on the 2009 Utah football team came from 2 Timothy 1:7. We began each class by repeating the scripture together: "For God hath not given us the spirit of fear; but of power, and of love, and of a sound mind." The team understood that fear is the opposite of hope and belief, and it relates to far more things in life than football.

I've seen hundreds of students in love over the years who allowed their belief and hope in their new mate to turn to a paralyzing fear of the unknown. They then allowed themselves to take counsel from these fears and started to doubt themselves and the relationship. Many of them fled the stadium before the game was over and ended promising relationships. We should enter into a loving relationship with both eyes wide open and seek the guidance of the Spirit to see through counterfeit imposters of mature and pure love. But once the Spirit has confirmed our choice and there is no new evidence to the contrary, why allow the spirit of fear into our lives?

In Paul's letter to Timothy, he explains that the spirit of fear certainly does not come from God. The last thing Satan wants is for couples to go to a temple of the Lord and to be endowed with the power to withstand his temptations. "God has not given us the spirit of fear" (2 Timothy 1:7), so such a spirit has to come from another source.

The Gifts of Power, Love, and a Sound Mind

Paul explained that if we can overcome our fears, then God can give us three gifts that strengthen our hope and belief and thus our ability to succeed. The first gift is power, which I believe is the power of the Holy Ghost bestowed upon those obedient to God's will. This greatest of all gifts gives us perfect hope in our abilities to solve problems and overcome any obstacle. Unfortunately, Satan knows perfectly well that fear cancels out the power of the Spirit and thus will do all he can to make us doubt.

The second gift is love. When we show that we love God and our fellow man and receive the power of the Holy Ghost, we then qualify for the third gift, a sound mind. I believe a sound mind to be a gift of the Spirit. It is the ability to think clearly under pressure and to find ways to solve life's problems. Belief and hope cause us to focus on the task at hand and open our mind to the correct course of action. Fear blocks out the Spirit's ability to teach us, making a sound mind impossible to achieve.

In chapter four, I gave the example of the wife whose husband was trying to cheat her out of her half of their assets while having an affair with a coworker. That situation is an example of this principle. When the wife was taking counsel from the spirit of fear, she was being led to only one solution to the problem, which was to get a lawyer. When she listened to and felt the power of the Spirit telling her not to let the marriage die and to go save her wayward husband, her sound mind was quickened and she saw another alternative that eventually saved their marriage.

A good scriptural account of hope versus fear comes from Paul's description of Abraham's test of faith in Romans 4:18–20. Abraham had been promised that he would be the father of many nations, yet he was close to a hundred years old. It must have seemed like it was time to mentally leave the stadium and give up hope and belief in this promised blessing. His elderly wife was no spring chicken either—it certainly looked like game over. These facts would cause most of us to lose hope and take counsel from our fears.

Paul said of Abraham: "*Who against hope believed in hope*, that he might become the father of many nations, according to that which was spoken, So shall thy seed be. And being not weak in faith, he considered not his own body now dead, when he was about an hundred years old, neither yet the deadness of Sara's womb: He staggered not at the promise of God through unbelief; *but was strong in faith*, giving glory to God" (Romans 4:18–20; emphasis added).

How many of us can "against hope" still believe in our imperfect family relations? There is great power in positive thinking. Belief and hope can lead to the faith that precedes miracles. It can happen in sports, so it can happen in love and in the home.

Rejoiceth in the Truth

How important is truth in love and intimate relationships? It's important enough to be mentioned 115 times in the Old Testament, 109 in the New Testament, 75 times in the Book of Mormon, 69 times in the Doctrine and Covenants, and 12 times in the Pearl of Great Price. It's been preached about 995 times in general conference and the lyric "truth" is used 224 times in our hymnbook.

The Book of Mormon prophet Jacob tells us the origin of all truth, what it is used for, and what it is: "Behold, my brethren, he that prophesieth, let him prophesy to the understanding of men; *for the Spirit speaketh the truth and lieth not.* Wherefore, it speaketh of things *as they really are*, and *of things as they really will be*; wherefore, these things are manifested unto us *plainly, for the salvation of our souls*" (Jacob 4:13; emphasis added).

Jacob taught that truth makes our communications understandable, is discovered and manifested by the Spirit, and never lies. Further, he said that truth consists of things as they really are (here and now) and really will be (in the future). The Doctrine and Covenants adds one more dimension to Jacob's definition of truth. It also is things as they really were (an accurate history of past events with no revisionism): "And truth is knowledge of things as they are, and *as they were*, and as they are to come" (D&C 93:24; emphasis added). Unless truth is the uncompromised standard in any intimate relationship, our ability to understand and trust each other can never be mastered and true, eternal love will never be built.

The LDS hymnbook celebrates truth in the song, "Oh Say, What Is Truth?" Look up the lyrics and think of them and truth's importance to love and marriage.

Unfortunately, not everyone values truth as much as the Lord does. We live in a day and age where many young adults believe in moral relativism, or (in the older term) situational ethics. I discussed this previously. There is a battle going on today as civilizations are trying to determine if there is such a thing as truth, or if we have to be governed by it. If this naïve attitude and belief system is carried into intimate relationships, the results are disastrous at each stage.

In dating, the first lie often ends the game before it has a chance to mature. No one wants to be married to someone untrustworthy. Honesty is important if we ever expect a relationship to move toward complete unity and to last throughout eternity.

The Truth and Questions to Ask before a Third Date

One returned sister missionary explained her rules of dating to our institute marriage class. Each of her rules dealt with truth and honesty, in one form or another. They were all based on her dating experiences and all came as a result of several difficult broken relationships.

She told the class that before she would go on a third date with any young man, she asked three questions. First, "Do you have another girlfriend?" She had once dated a young man for three months and thought they were getting serious when he announced one night that this would be the last date because he was getting married in ten days and had a lot of things to do. Was it dishonest of the young man to act in this way? All the women reading this are probably thinking, *Are you kidding?* (Many of the young men reading this are likely still thinking about it.)

Her second question was, "Are you a gamer?" She found she didn't want to compete with anyone's online gaming addiction ever again. Is it dishonest for young men to withhold such information? My answer is that it is dishonest to withhold any information about your behavior that can negatively impact the relationship, whether or not they are likely to find out about it later. Get it out and deal with it. Start your relationship off as Adam and Eve did in the Garden of Eden: naked (metaphorically) with nothing to hide (Genesis 2:25).

Her third question was, "Are you addicted to pornography?" If the answer is no, she provided a follow-up question: "Have you ever been addicted to pornography?" If the answer is yes, then, "How long has it been since your last relapse?" Her advice was that your potential mate should be free for at least a year before you commit to moving forward.

Some of my other students felt she should have added two additional questions: "Do you have a current temple recommend?" "Do you have a job or are you making progress toward a career that will provide security for a future family?"

Gray Areas of Honesty

The need for honesty never ends in a relationship. However, there are differing opinions on what honesty includes. Not all situations are as black and white as a young husband who bought a new truck and hid it at the neighbors' house each night. (His wife only discovered it when the insurance bill came.)

I often tell my students in marriage classes about an incident in my own marriage and ask them if I was honest or not. I tell them I think I have never lied to my wife, but then add that my wife may have a different opinion.

I tell them my wife and I were having a spirited discussion about who was the best driver. It started with me asking her why she tailgates slow drivers. She replied it encourages them to speed up. I said that she was risking a wreck. She said that women's reflexes are faster than men's and that's why so many more women can get away with it and men can't. I asked if that was why she has had six wrecks in forty years and I had none. My logic failed to win the day and we dropped it before I lost dinner. The next day on the way to work, a young driver slammed on her brakes as a stoplight turned yellow. I was expecting her to just go through the light, so I had to slam on my brakes in response. Unfortunately, I was on a patch of frost on the road and slid into her rear bumper at probably five miles an hour.

My first accident had come within twelve hours of bragging to my wife that I had never been in one. The damage to the other car was minimal and my insurance company took care of everything. The damage to my Jeep Wrangler was only a bent bumper, so I went to the Jeep dealer and bought a new bumper and put it on myself before my wife got home. I put the old damaged bumper in the attic and "forgot" about the incident.

Several months later, my wife discovered the old bumper in the attic and asked me what it was. I replied it looked like an old Jeep bumper. Wives are not stupid, mine particularly. She figured out the whole thing in just a few seconds, quickly recalled our best-driver debate and entered into a discussion about what is and isn't a lie. I seldom get any of my female students to see my manly logic in this story, but there are always a few men who will side with me.

My wife and I do agree that honesty is necessary as an environment for pure love to grow in. Lies drive the light away. The truth sets us free and helps us grow in love. Honest couples tell the truth and appreciate the great blessing of trust in each other. It's that simple.

Black and White Areas of Honesty: Adultery and Infidelity

Another aspect of honesty in this section is the expectation of exclusivity that every marriage should have when couples marry. In a traditional marriage, when one of the partners engages in sexual relations outside of that marriage, it is often called cheating, and for good reason. It is the ultimate form of dishonesty and destroys true love in a similar manner to the way stepping on a land mine in a minefield can wound or maim a solder.

In relating marriage to this metaphor, married couples are walking toward their destination and one of them steps on a mine, thereby injuring everyone close by. Sometimes they can be healed, but the damage is substantial in every case. Here are a few Kinsey research findings on how prevalent these mines are in serious relationships:

- Infidelity has been found to be the single most cited cause of divorce in over 150 cultures.[34]
- In Western countries, 25–50 percent of divorcees cite a spouse's infidelity as the primary cause of the divorce.[35]

- Approximately 50 percent of divorced men and women reported that their former spouse had engaged in extra-marital sex.[36]
- Approximately 20–25 percent of men and 10–15 percent of women engage in extramarital sex at least once during their marriage.[37]
- Women are less approving than men of sexual justifications for extramarital affairs, preferring emotional reasons such as "falling in love."[38]
- Around 11 percent of adults who have ever been married or cohabited have been unfaithful to their partners.[39]

Respondents who reported that their relationships were "pretty happy" and "not too happy" were two and four times more likely, respectively, to have reported extramarital sex than respondents who reported that they were "very happy" with their relationships.[40]

By 2011, there were strong indications that America's descent down this slippery slope may be accelerating. With the fight to modify the legal definition of marriage has come the fight to decide if there are such things as moral standards.

The attempts to remove nuptial boundaries on monogamy have increased. It is almost as though Korihor (Alma 30) himself has come back from the dead and is selling his distorted message in the mainstream media. His message is essentially that monogamy harms relationships and is dishonest. Korihor's doctrine portrays infidelity as glamorous, exciting, and the antidote for repressed, frustrated, and sexually boring relationships.

I have counseled many couples who believed in this false doctrine and tried it out, only to learn the hard way that wickedness never was happiness. Their stories are sad, and the effect on their relationships and lives is devastating.

I have worked with enough bad examples in my lifetime to say that even if I totally lost faith in God and in all religious principles, I would still live a chaste life. I say this because I have witnessed the total misery that cheating brings to anyone who does it, whether they believe in God and His laws about chastity or not. Like any law of nature, we cannot break the law of chastity; we can only break ourselves against it.

The greatest tragedy that comes from this folly is not necessarily the obvious physical results such as sexually transmitted diseases, poverty, or disadvantaged children that come from divorce, as sad and serious as these are. The greatest harm comes from the loss of ever finding true love and achieving our divine destiny.

Deceived people who seek happiness from hedonism lose any hope of ever finding true, pure, and eternal love. It's a sad irony and the natural consequence of abandoning the "great plan of happiness" (Alma 42:16). By trying to substitute God's plan with Satan's hedonism, we lose the capacity for feeling and for happiness, just like how the father of lies has lost his capacity for happiness. So "he seeketh that all men might be miserable like unto himself" (2 Nephi 2:27).

Summary

This chapter began by asking the question, "How do we better demonstrate love in non-demanding, self-sacrificing, everyday actions that are appreciated by those we love and ultimately bring us to greater unity?"

Next, we examined Moroni's counsel that the ability to experience true love is a gift that is bestowed upon the obedient. "With this love, which he hath bestowed upon all who *are true followers* of his Son, Jesus Christ." This gift of true love has at least three prerequisite requirements we must master before we can attempt to apply the rest of the program: meekness (or humility), faith, and hope.

We then introduced Moroni's thirteen-part answer to this question. This chapter discussed eight of the thirteen traits that we can use to master the art of true love: suffereth long; beareth all things; endureth all things; is not easily provoked; is Kind; believeth all things; hopeth all things; and rejoiceth in the truth.

Applying True Love Self-Evaluation Questions—Part 1

- How would you rate your mastery of the true love foundation prerequisites of faith, hope, and humility?
  A. I have great faith, hope, and sufficient humility
  B. Average
  C. Less than I need

- How well do you endure trouble, opposition, or anguish without becoming angry (easily provoked), frustrated, or overly anxious?
  A. I am nearly always under control
  B. I have some room for improvement
  C. I have a lot of room for improvement
- How much patience and endurance do you have in accepting God's will and His timing in answers to earnest prayer?
  A. Complete patience
  B. I have room for improvement
  C. Less than I need
- How patient are you in the smaller, less dramatic, everyday experiences with your companion?
  A. They hardly ever bother me
  B. Sometimes they get to me
  C. They bother me most of the time
- How much "long suffering" and tolerance do you have with all people? Can you tolerate their imperfections?
  A. Most always
  B. Usually
  C. I'm rather critical most of the time
- Can you tolerate your own imperfections as you work to overcome faults and weaknesses?
  A. Yes
  B. Usually
  C. Hardly ever
- Are you able to or will you be able to accept the normal physical changes of your spouse's appearance as they age?
  A. Yes, completely
  B. Usually, but sometimes it bothers me
  C. It bothers me
- People who know me are likely to describe me as kind, pleasant, tender, concerned for others, and possessing a mild disposition.
  A. Most people would think of me like this
  B. At least half would do so
  C. Hardly anyone would describe me this way

- I view marriage (relationships) with optimism, trust, and a determination to solve our problems, *or* . . . I view marriage (relationships) with optimism, trust, and a determination to someday be able to solve problems.
  A. Most of the time
  B. About half the time
  C. Usually I view it with pessimism and distrust, and I easily give up when problems arise
- Truth and honesty are both extremely important to me in relationships.
  A. Always
  B. Usually
  C. Not really
- I am able to bridle inappropriate sexual thoughts or temptations about anyone I am not married to and can quickly return to a controlled mental state.
  A. Always
  B. Nearly always
  C. I need to improve here
- I avoid situations that can compromise my moral integrity and lead me down the road to eventually cheating on my spouse or fiancé or partner or a future relationship.
  A. Always
  B. Nearly always
  C. I need to improve here

Chapter 8: Applying True Love Principles-Part 2

S uccessful marriages and families are established and maintained by correctly applying true principles of love.

Things Not to Do in Any Relationship

This chapter presents seven things from Moroni's list that destroy pure love and respect in all relationships and are to be avoided: "And charity . . . envieth not, and is not puffed up, seeketh not her own, is not easily provoked, thinketh no evil, and rejoiceth not in iniquity" (Moroni 7:45). One of my theories on the foundations of a strong marriage is that we should constantly evaluate our relationships and look to increase the things we do that our partner enjoys (and that increases respect) while at the same time trying to discover and eliminate behaviors that our partner dislikes (and that creates disrespect). Chapter seven presented Moroni's list of positive things that lead to an increase in respect and therefore love. This chapter will discuss Moroni's list of negative behaviors that we should strive to eliminate if we want to find and keep eternal love.

Envieth Not

The first negative on Moroni's list is "envieth not." There are several examples of envy in the scriptures that led to marital and family discord. In Genesis 30:1, Rachel was envious of her sister Leah's ability to produce children and she subsequently projected her anger onto her husband. She demanded, "Jacob, give me children, or else I die." Frustrated, Jacob responded as most men would—with anger and defensiveness to this ultimatum, born of envy: "Am I in God's stead, who hath withheld from thee the fruit of the womb?" Jacob and Rachel's prayers were eventually answered with the late arrival of their son Joseph. Ironically, favored child Joseph later became a victim of envy himself when his half-brothers sold him into slavery (see Acts 7:9).

Looking to the Book of Mormon, Nephi's life certainly would have been simpler if his older brothers hadn't been consumed with a similar murderous envy. You don't have to be in an intimate relationship to have envy ruin relationships with friends, siblings, coworkers, teammates, and so on. Additionally, you don't need to have a famous spouse to experience envy in a relationship. Consider the following admission of a newlywed wife:

> I realize that I need to work on not being envious of my husband's successes and opportunities and should just support him and rejoice in his happiness. My husband is currently working at a hospital and going to school full-time (twenty-three credit hours). Additionally, he is able to handle all of this and still get really good grades. I have been struggling to find a job for the past two years because of my hard school schedule and I struggle to keep my GPA up. So sometimes I get jealous of my husband for being so successful. On top of all that, when he gets home from school and work, he is always in a good mood and proceeds to take care of me by making dinner or cleaning up. He really is my superman. But sometimes I feel so incredibly weak next to him. He is so strong and easygoing and I struggle to handle stress. Sometimes his crazy life takes precedence over mine and I get jealous of all the attention that we spend on him and his problems. I know that if the roles were reversed, he would look at me with pride and rejoice in my successes. I am trying hard to do the same for him. I need to realize that he loves sharing his successes with me and that when he succeeds, I succeed, and vice versa.

This young woman, after talking about her problem, provides the solution at the end of her story, one that basically solves the envy problem in all marriages: "I need to realize . . . that when he succeeds, I succeed, and vice versa." This is not as easy as it sounds. Mankind is jealous and competitive by nature. That weakness can easily find its way into any marriage or relationship unless we learn to "overcome the natural man" (Mosiah 3:19). Overcoming our envy is essential to becoming one with an eternal mate.

In-Law Envy

There's a particular relationship that my students have reported on frequently in my classes. I've heard their complaints so many times over the years that I think it bears mentioning here. The relationship is either (and most often) the new wife to her mother-in-law, the new husband to his mother-in-law, or (far less often) father-in-law to daughter- or son-in-law. Some of my students say these relationships are strained and difficult at best. I've listened to their stories (some of which can only be described as horror stories), and I have concluded that there are many dynamics at play here.

The one relationship I'm most familiar with is that of my wife and my mother. They were best of friends and got along fabulously. I also loved my wife's parents and her siblings and extended family. I've seen many other families that learn to love all the in-laws, so sometimes I wonder why we can't all just get along. Why should there be any contention among in-laws in Latter-day Saint homes where we are challenged to learn, live, and share the gospel? How bad can it get? The following are three dramatic examples from among the dozens I've heard through my students:

One future mother-in-law was so distraught at the thought of losing her son that, out of panic, she repeatedly rammed her son's car with her SUV so he and his fiancée couldn't drive to the airport to make their flight to meet the fiancée's parents. When the trunk popped open from the assault, she also took their luggage. The couple still managed to make the flight and later marry, and the mother-in-law eventually softened her resistance. They have since then learned to get along.

The second example is a mother-in-law who announced to her new son-in-law that she was taking her daughter back just two months after the temple marriage. She said this was because he had changed his college major and she did not approve of the new career choice. The daughter resisted until her mother took her on an expensive shopping trip and told her she had to choose between her family and her new husband. This example does not have a happy ending as the new bride ended up chosing her mother's pressure and bribes over her temple marriage.

The third example is of a daughter-in-law who, after several years of marriage, demanded that her husband cut off all contact with his entire extended family. She did this in an attempt to use his parents and siblings as hostages in a power struggle to control all aspects of their marriage.

These examples all have common factors. They defy logic and normal reasoning powers and drive charity and the principles upon which true love is based right out the front door of the home. They invite the spirit of contention to come in and take their place. In-law relationships have the ability to produce strong emotions that drive the Spirit away, destroy normal brain function, and turn us into people that we never thought we could become. Afterward, many of us find ways to justify these non-civil, non-gospel-based changes in our lives and stubbornly refuse to repent. Really, why can't we all just get along?

One of the reasons contentions happen so often in these relationships is because of envy (though we could also include competition, pride, and selfishness here just as well). Some parents just can't let go of their children, are envious of this new person in their children's lives, and interfere more than they should with new marriages. Some sons and daughters can't let go of their parents and encourage the interference, especially if it involves receiving money. Some new husbands or wives become envious of the entire extended family of their spouse and choose to compete rather than find ways to cooperate, share, be fair, or compromise. Again, why can't we all just get along?

Three scriptures can help in developing a general principle to get along with in-laws:

- "Therefore shall a man leave his father and his mother, and shall cleave unto his wife: and they shall be one flesh" (Genesis 2:24). This scripture is fairly clear where our priorities should be placed. All new marriages are important to the survival of the human race and need room to grow. Mothers and fathers do their best parenting when they prepare their children to form new and independent unions of their own. Does this mean that after their children are married, their job is done? Well, yes and no.

- The second scripture says, "Honour thy father and thy mother: that thy days may be long upon the land which the Lord thy God giveth thee" (Exodus 20:12). This verse says nothing about the commandment being revoked once the child is married. It's a delicate balance that newlyweds must make in seeking the counsel and wisdom gained by experience from their parents while learning to work things out on our own. Parents need to tread carefully in the garden of their married children's new lives, helping them to grow rather than carelessly stepping on the new plants and then hoping they can recover from the interference. Envy, competition, and pride can quickly destroy this delicate balance and our ability to tread lightly. These feelings can cause us to do and say things totally out of place, resulting in lost opportunities for receiving or giving counsel, friendships, many positive experiences, and loving relationships.

- The third scripture is explained by President Gordon B. Hinckley in the April 1998 general conference (in his talk enititled "We Bear Witness of Him"): "Let us be true disciples of the Christ, observing the Golden Rule, doing unto others as we would have them do unto us." If we were all true disciples of Jesus Christ and lived consistently by the Golden Rule, in-law problems would go away and we truly would all get along just fine.

Prosperity and Fame Envy

Another harmful use of envy today is detailed in Psalm 73:3: "For I was envious at the foolish, when I saw the prosperity of the wicked." How many people dive into financial hot water by borrowing far beyond their means because they are envious of those around them who appear to be wealthier? Elder Dallin H. Oaks of the Quorum of the Twelve Apostles warned against this type of envy of the wealth of others, saying, "A person who covets the wealth of another will suffer spiritually."[41]

Proverbs 14:30 provides an interesting comparison that effectively sums up the harmfulness of envy: "A sound heart is the life of the flesh: but envy the rottenness of the bones." Just as the heart pumps life-giving blood to the flesh, envy has a similar power to figuratively bring rottenness to our bones. It's a great analogy of what envy can do to any kind of relationship.

Envy is the opposite of true love. Perfect love rejoices in another's successes. In marriage, love supports one other's important interests, activities, and callings, celebrating their talents. Pure love never compares one eternal companion to another. Envy, jealousy, scorekeeping, and covetousness have no place in a home filled with mature love. The same can be said for most kinds of relationships. Envy kills harmony and good will.

I've often wondered how much truth there is to a line that I heard in a movie about a famous but frustrated country singer who lamented that a person could have fame or have love, but not both. The fact that Moroni warned us about envy may lend some support to that idea. It may also help explain why many Hollywood celebrity marriages have such short lifespans.

If marriage partners gain some fame and their mates see them as getting more attention, the neglected mates often feel they are always getting cold standing in the shadows. Therefore, it's not surprising when those in the shadows start seeking warmth somewhere else, or when those in the sunlight forget that there is someone always standing in their shadows. What can be done about the fame-envy problem?

The fame problem is mentioned in Doctrine and Covenants 121. For the most part, the scripture refers to priesthood leaders who allow the prestige of their callings to overshadow the need for humility and qualifying for the Spirit to guide them in doing God's work. However, you can also read it with the "famous partner syndrome" in mind and it works just as well. Substitute fame for both authority and priesthood and apply it to an intimate relationship, and we have a model for perfect love behavior, when one's partner or friends achieve success in life:

> We have learned by sad experience that it is the nature and disposition of almost all men, as soon as they get a little authority [or fame], as they suppose, they will immediately begin to exercise unrighteous dominion. Hence many are called, but few are chosen. No power or influence

can or ought to be maintained by virtue of the priesthood [or becoming famous], only by persuasion, by long-suffering, by gentleness and meekness, and by love unfeigned; By kindness, and pure knowledge, which shall greatly enlarge the soul without hypocrisy, and without guile. (D&C 121:39–42)

It's important for everyone to do his or her best to make his or her mate or friend feel significant, respected, and completely equal in the relationship. Paul explained this principle in a letter to the Corinthians: "And the eye cannot say unto the hand, I have no need of thee: nor again the head to the feet, I have no need of you" (1 Corinthians 12:21). The greater the fame, the more effort should be made to make partners, friends, and so on feel just as important in the relationship.

In marriage, this needs to happen when one partner's contribution to the marriage may result in bringing in far more money (or all of the money), receives a leadership position in the Church or community, or gains more esteem, prestige, and notoriety in the eyes of the world for whatever reason.

I have a good friend who was called as a mission president. Before their mission, he was the breadwinner with a prestigious education and profession while his wife chose to be a stay-at-home mom. They served faithfully together with the husband presiding in the mission and his wife serving alongside of him, completely supporting him while fulfilling her own duties. They worked as a team with no jealousy or envy, just as they had always done. They continued to see themselves as equals with separate duties and completed a successful mission.

Not long after their return, the husband retired and the wife was called to a high position in the Church. Now it was the husband's turn to be supportive with no jealousy or envy while his wife became the one in the spotlight of fame. He responded with perfect charity as she fulfilled her duties of speaking in meetings and traveling throughout the world. Shortly after her release, the husband became physically incapacitated and it was again her turn to sacrifice and be supportive. Throughout all their changes in circumstance, they always saw each as equals and treated one another with respect.

It is important for the less-famed partner to try and stay on the high road and conscientiously follow Moroni's counsel to "envieth not."

Everyone needs to learn to accept and appreciate what each partner does for the good of the relationship. Perceived fame is a fleeting thing and circumstances can and do change quickly. More is said about this part of envy in the next section, where we examine envy's first cousin, pride.

Is Not Puffed Up

Strong's *Concordance with Hebrew and Greek Lexicon* lists *proud* and *arrogant* as translations of "puffed up." It is a descriptive phrase used six times in the New Testament and eight times in the Book of Mormon. Half of the uses of "puffed up" in Book of Mormon are as part of prophesies of people's behavior in our time: the last days. How is it possible for these ancient prophets to have seen such detail in our lives? Mormon told us, "Behold, I speak unto you as if ye were present, and yet ye are not. But behold, Jesus Christ hath shown you unto me, and I know your doing" (Mormon 8:35). These prophets saw our lives and the times we live in long before we were born.

Types of Prideful Behavior That Harm Relationships

Pride includes such things as "self-centeredness, conceit, boastfulness, arrogance, or haughtiness."[42] Some of these conditions are capable of delivering a knockout blow to the relationship during the eternal mate selection process. However, President Ezra Taft Benson said that these are certainly elements of the sin, but are not the heart of it.[43] The heart of pride is apparently inappropriate competitiveness that leads to enmity. *Enmity* is a feeling or condition of hostility, hatred, ill will, animosity, and antagonism.

The first form of this enmity is hatred toward and rebellion against God Himself. Pride leads us to a belief that "nobody can tell me what to do." If we feel that way about God and His commandments, what chance does our partner have of influencing our behavior for the better? (See the classic example of Korihor in Alma 30 for enmity against God.) If we find ourselves rebelling against and competing with our mate instead of seeking unity, there is a good chance pride has crept in the back door and is camped out in the home.

In marriage, pride stops us from trying to seek a celestial state of cooperation and collaboration, or at least a terrestrial level of compromise. Instead, the proud stubbornly stick to their telestial guns and try to defeat their eternal mates through some form of marital combat. President Bensons stated that if this competition occurs, then we often have "allowed our desires, appetites, and passions to go unbridled,"[44] and this can be the gateway to a variety of additional sinful and harmful behaviors that have the potential to utterly destroy our relationships.

The proud can convince themselves that there is no real harm in viewing pornography or taking addictive substances or listening to inappropriate media, yet I've seen each of these unbridled passions and appetites break up dating couples and eternal marriages. Pride makes us vulnerable to the great deceiver, which makes it possible for him to "deceive the very elect, who are the elect according to the covenant" (Joseph Smith—Matthew 1:22).

The oft-committed sin of enmity toward God manifests itself in many other ways in intimate relationships. These include such relationship and marriage-destroying actions as rebellion against a mate's desires or needs just to prove our own stubborn independence. Our pride can lead us to be unrepentant just to prove we answer to no one—not our in-laws, not the Church, not God, and especially not our partner.

The proud are quite easily offended and ultra-sensitive to their perceived inadequacies. They relish the victim role and could often be nominated for the best actor or actress in a dramatic courtship or marriage.

In April 1989, President Ezra Taft Benson opened many of our eyes to a different type of pride in his talk entitled "Beware of Pride." He called it "pride from the bottom looking up." It shows up in relationships as "faultfinding, gossiping, backbiting, murmuring, living beyond our means, envying, coveting, withholding gratitude and praise that might lift another, and being unforgiving and jealous." All of these prideful behaviors have their beginnings in competitively comparing ourselves to others and becoming angry because they have something we think we don't. These behaviors have the potential to destroy any kind of relationship and have no place in the lives of those seeking a love that will last throughout eternity.

One of the most common forms of pride in any courtship and marriage is the classic power struggle where a man and a woman engage in battle to see whose desires will prevail. They do this because neither partner wants to be controlled by the other, so they engage in an emotional battle in an attempt to hang onto their independence and rugged individualism.

These couples usually end up settling on one of two approaches: an evasive approach to their self-centered rebellion and unwillingness to compromise (in what psychologist John Gottman called subtly hostile and detached); or they become hostile and engaged,[45] using temper tantrums and anger to have their way and make sure no one ever rules over them. This type of a combative environment makes it difficult for love to grow and relationships to prosper. It has no place in the new and everlasting covenant of marriage.

All forms of contention have their roots in pride. This includes arguments, unrighteous dominion, abuse, and John Gottman's four horsemen of the apocalypse: "criticism, contempt, defensiveness, and stonewalling."[46] Using these behaviors or refusing to change our minds in the face of obvious truth all fall under the category of pride.

The Antidote for Pride

There are a multitude of ways pride can destroy eternal relationships. Each of these ugly manifestations of cancerous pride has an antidote. We examined the causes of pride and how it evolves previously. This chapter will discuss how we can overcome pride by first recognizing that we have it and understanding what it does to relationships. We then vow to choose to be humble instead by "swallowing our pride." We do so by realizing there is equality in true love and no entitlements because of our gender or supposed fame, accomplishments, or positions. Humility leads us to apologize when we make a mistake. Admitting our mistakes is not a sign of weakness; it is just the opposite.

An attitude of gratitude is another antidote for pride. Gratitude keeps our blessings in perspective and helps us realize all our blessings ultimately come from God's grace and condescension. This realization should teach us that our own skill and wisdom is nothing without the gifts given us by our Creator. This truth should help keep us humble and our pride in check.

Another great antidote for pride is compassion. If we follow the Savior's example of "having the bowels of mercy; being filled with compassion towards the children of men" (Mosiah 15:9; see also 3 Nephi 17:6–7; 1 John 3:17), then there is no room left for performance-killing pride in our lives. Pride is always competitive, disrespectful, and leads to meanness and putting others down. Compassion brings out the opposite in us. Much more will be said about the exalting principle of compassion in chapter nine.

Seeketh Not Her [or His] Own

The Topical Guide cross-reference for this scripture (Moroni 7:45) is *selfishness*. We can build a case that selfishness is caused by pride and therefore falls underneath its broad umbrella. However, both the Apostle Paul and Moroni felt that selfishness was a sin grievous enough to discuss in a category by itself, so we will do the same.

Unselfishness is the best manifestation of humility and a broken heart and contrite spirit. If pride is best characterized by enmity and rebellion toward God, then unselfishness is best manifested by our love of God through keeping His commandments and loving our fellow man as we love ourselves (see Matthew 22).

In 1976, President Spencer W. Kimball gave us a list of types of behavior in marriage that constitute unselfishness:

> But it [marriage] means sacrifice, sharing, and even a reduction of some personal liberties. . . . It means long, hard economizing. . . . It means children who bring with them financial burdens, service burdens, care and worry burdens; but also it means the deepest and sweetest emotions of all. . . . Sweethearts should realize before they take the vows that each must accept literally and fully that the good of the little new family must always be superior to the good of either spouse. . . . Each party must eliminate the "I" and the "my" and substitute therefore "we" and "our.". . . . Every decision must take into consideration that there are two or more affected by it.[47]

President Kimball then summed up the whole ongoing problem of divorce by telling us what its foundation consists of: "Every divorce is the result of selfishness on the part of one or the other or both parties to a marriage contract."

Where Is Selfishness Taking Us?

The Apostle Paul said of life in the last days, "This know also, that in the last days perilous times shall come. For men shall be lovers of their own selves" (2 Timothy 3:1–2). To be lovers of our own selves is to be selfish. If, as President Kimball suggested, every divorce is the result of selfishness, then today's high divorce rates indicate we are certainly in the last days spoken of by Paul. Selfishness may also explain other changes in the way many in the world currently look at marriage, divorce, children, and family life.

Some research[48] reports dramatic increases in the following: divorce rates, number of children of divorce, those over eighteen who have never married, those with negative attitudes about marriage, couples living together outside of marriage, unmarried couples raising children, uncommitted couples with children, higher marriage ages, unwed mothers, abortion rates, adultery, fatherless homes, crime, mothers who are in the labor force, and same-sex unions.

At the same time, there have been dramatic decreases in the following: traditional moral and ethical standards, birthrates, those with an optimistic view of the institution of marriage and the family, fidelity in marriage, teens with positive attitudes about marriage and family, child-centeredness in families, and overall family well-being.

Perhaps cofounding editors David Popenoe and Barbara Dafoe Whitehead best predicted the future in 1999 in the first of "The State of Our Unions" reports, giving commentary on marriage and family life in America. They warned family scholars, the media, government, and the public about "the rise among young adults of sex without strings, relationships without rings."[49]

Numerous young single men today seem particularly smitten with the selfishness bug, according to the report. The 2002 "State of Our Unions" report by the National Marriage Project examined reasons why men won't commit. Barbara Dafoe Whitehead and David Popenoe summarized those findings: "A special essay on young, not-yet married men's attitudes on the timing of marriage finds that men experience few social pressures to marry, gain many of the benefits of marriage by cohabiting with a romantic partner, and are ever more reluctant to commit to marriage in their early adult years."[50]

I believe most of these destabilizing and (according to the family proclamation) civilization-threatening[51] changes have come about because old-fashioned selfishness has been repackaged and relabeled with such modern, popular, secular, and politically correct terms as personal happiness, individual and personal freedoms, liberation, adult-centered, career-centered, personal growth, self-improvement, self-growth, self-fulfillment, self-gratification, and self-seeking—all of which sound a lot like self-centeredness.

The Unsought Consequences of Selfishness

One of the greatest examples of selfishness in our modern world may be the devaluation of children that has led one social scientist to suggest that "the most important change that has occurred in the modern American family seems to be from child centered to adult centered."[52] The result of this adult-centeredness is fewer children, an aging population, and many neglected children who are not prepared to economically contribute to society.

Do the scriptures say anything about selfishness in the last days? Look at how the Lord describes our times in Doctrine and Covenants and decide for yourself:

> And the anger of the Lord is kindled, and his sword is bathed in heaven, and it shall fall upon the inhabitants of the earth. And the arm of the Lord shall be revealed; and the day cometh that they who will not hear the voice of the Lord, neither the voice of his servants, neither give heed to the words of the prophets and apostles, shall be cut off from among the people; For they have strayed from mine ordinances, and have broken mine everlasting covenant [enmity toward God]; *they seek not the Lord to establish his righteousness, but every man walketh in his own way, and after the image of his own god, whose image is in the likeness of the world* [enmity toward fellow man], and whose substance is that of an idol, which waxeth old and shall perish in Babylon, even Babylon the great, which shall fall. (D&C 1:13–16; emphasis added)

The Lord's message is clear: "A self-centered society is unsustainable." No one can find true love that lasts for eternity without first learning to bridle his or her selfishness.

Thinketh No Evil

The next thing to avoid on Moroni's list is to think no evil. "As [a man] thinketh in his heart, so is he" (Proverbs 23:7). Negative speaking always flows from negative thinking. The words we say to each other have the potential to raise each other to new heights or sink us into the depths of despair. All evil communications have their origins in uncontrolled, malicious, and unconstructive thoughts.

Years ago in a counseling setting, a young woman came to me for help with her marriage. For over an hour, she let forth a constant barrage of recalled disappointments and frustrations she had experienced with her husband during their ten years of marriage. She released a great deal of pent-up frustration. Finally, I asked her to count her negative thoughts about her husband for the next three days so we could establish a baseline for this behavior. I asked her to carry three-by-five cards and make a tic mark to record each negative thought.

She came back a week later and reported she averaged over 1,200 negative thoughts a *day* about her husband. Some scientists have theorize that the average person thinks about 12,000 thoughts per day. To have 10 percent of those be negative thoughts about her husband, the woman would have to be consumed with anger, bitterness, and a contentious spirit.

Her husband had become her intimate enemy and the center of her conscious thought patterns for much of each day. She watched him intently and noted every action that could be possibly seen in a negative light. This great evil was eating away at the foundation of their marriage.

I asked her if she was committed to saving her marriage. She paused, but then said she was. I asked her to make a list of ten things she admired about her husband. She had a hard time doing this as she had learned to block out all his positive traits and to ignore all his positive behaviors.

She had to look at wedding and honeymoon pictures and read old love letters and her early personal journal entries to finally come up with a list. I then asked her to prioritize and memorize the list. She did so.

Her next assignment was to recall and mentally recite the list of his good traits every time she had a negative thought about her husband. It was a variation of stopping and counting to ten as a way to cut off the fuse to her anger before detonation.

Similar to professional athletes who discipline their minds so that they can eliminate any performance-destroying negative thoughts, this woman also retrained her mind to view her husband in a better light. She started to notice and appreciate the positive things he did for her and the family. This alone didn't solve all their problems, but it did help create a non-toxic environment where the problems had a chance of being solved.

Entropy

How does someone go from a young bride or groom so deeply in love and so totally positive in their mind-set about their new mate that they literally see no evil or the slightest flaw to thinking 1,200 or more negative thoughts a day about his or her mate a mere ten years later?

An answer can actually be found in comparing marital relationships to a simplified explanation of the laws of classical thermodynamics developed in the early 1800s. Take the example of an air-conditioned room in Houston, Texas, in August. If you have ever been to Houston in August, this example will immediately make sense to you, though the example of a cold climate works just as well. Without air conditioning, the room temperature of homes often rises to a muggy and uncomfortable ninety or more degrees. With proper insulation and air conditioning, the temperature can be brought down to a comfortable seventy-two degrees. However, unless you live in a deep cave in the Houston area, achieving an inside-the-home temperature of seventy-two degrees is not a natural or easily achieved state. It takes a great deal of energy and maintenance to run the air conditioners and keep the homes cool.

The natural state is for the inside of the home to equalize with the hotter outside surroundings because the hostile outside environment is much greater in volume and pressure than the lesser thermodynamic system created by the boundary of the home's walls, roof, and insulation.

"Entropy is the only quantity in the physical sciences that seems to imply a particular direction of progress, sometimes called the arrow of time. As time progresses, the second law of thermodynamics states that the entropy of an isolated system never decreases."[53]

In other words, unless something is done to intervene in our physical world, everything reverts back to its most disorganized state. Turn off the air conditioning and the home gets hot. Stop watering, mowing, and fertilizing the lawn and it will turn into a brown, overgrown weed patch. Lie in a hospital bed for a month and walking becomes difficult. In our fallen, mortal world, we are required to work by the sweat of our brow and to weed, plow, plant, harvest, repair, pay the electric bill, and overcome entropy. Until we return to a Garden of Eden state, this is our plight.

Human relationships also experience entropy in a somewhat similar manner to the physical world around us. Some social scientists refer to it as social entropy. Social entropy is based on a doctrine of inevitable social decline and degeneration. These social scientists point out that entire nations and civilizations have predictably followed entropy's "arrow of time," all the way back to the dark ages.

The ancient Nephite and Lamanite societies constantly struggled with reverting back to a natural man state rather than an enlightened, refined, spiritually-based people. The ancient Romans and Greeks and other societies have followed similar paths of degeneration. We can easily see more recent examples of man's march from enlightenment to hedonism in our current society's efforts to redefine the family and accommodate both amoral and immoral belief systems.

Neither good friends nor intimate couples can really think these physical and societal entropy laws do *not* apply to their relationships or that they can neglect maintaining their bonds and still endure in happiness to the end. There is a hostile, love-destroying environment lurking just outside the walls of all couple's homes (and sometimes even inside the walls) that, because of its sheer volume, mass, and pressure, will overpower any couple that stops trying to fight it. Just as there is an air conditioning bill, there is also a marriage conditioning utility bill that must be paid regularly.

The degradation of a positive mind-set is one of the first sign of the onslaught of entropy's effects. No relationship can survive attacks of constant negative thinking and the resulting behaviors. It is not difficult to understand that the way we think about people will eventually influence the way we talk to them and decide to treat them, not to mention the quality of the relationship.

The Five-to-One Ratio

Researcher John Gottman found that healthy relationships need a five-to-one ratio of positive-to-negative communication to keep the effects of marital entropy at bay.[54] This positive communication can be anything from a smile and a nod to a hug to a rose, or even just a "You look great tonight." It's communication that "is kind" (see previous chapter) on Moroni's love-actions list. It's what President Gordon B. Hinckley called *civility*.

Notice that there is a one in the five-to-one ratio. We all manage to unknowingly irritate each other at times and will blissfully continue to do so unless our mate informs us about it. These experiences are called complaints. Complaints are not necessarily bad; for many couples, expressing concerns can help clear the air if communicated kindly by the offended partner. The scripture call it, "Reproving betimes with sharpness, when moved upon by the Holy Ghost" (D&C 121:43).

If offending partners or friends listen to and truly care about their partner's feelings and correct their behavior accordingly, then all is well and all the offended mate needs to do to balance things out is follow the scriptural admonition of "showing forth afterwards an increase of love toward him whom thou hast reproved, lest he esteem thee to be his enemy" (D&C 121:43). When we withdraw a complaint from our savings account and spend it on informing our partner about his or her faults, we need to deposit at least five kindnesses to make up for it and to assure our mate that this issue has done no permanent damage.

If offending partners—rather than listening to their partner's concerns about their differences and correcting the problem—choose to instead downplay its importance, or as King Benjamin called it: "to trifle with the words which I shall speak" (Mosiah 2:9), and do little to change or compromise, then we quickly enter the negativity cycle.

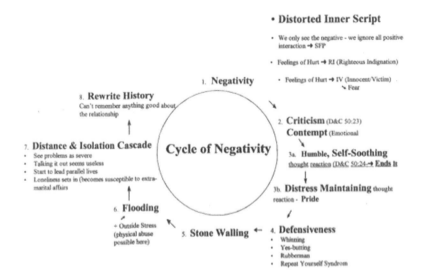

The Cycle of Negativity

According to Gottman,[55] when the positive-to-negative ratio dips far below the five-to-one ratio, eight predictable entropy events start to happen, which he calls "the cycle of negativity."

1. *Negativity:* In this form of entropy, a couple's "distorted inner script," or over-abundance of negative thoughts, starts to consume their relationship. I've seen this happen in pre-marriage and marriage relationships alike. It's called "distorted inner script" because the way they see things doesn't always match reality. They ignore the good things that happen in the relationship and instead wait like a cat lurking outside a mouse hole, ready to pounce on their unsuspecting victim the moment he or she comes into view.

When one mate makes the perceived mistake and the other mate's ultra-sensitive feelings are hurt, Gottman says the sensitive partner ambushes his or her spouse in one of three ways: either reacting with righteous indignation, playing the innocent victim role, or sometimes using a combination of both. I've seen these roles perfected so well that the actors could practically be nominated for an academy award.

When people are playing the innocent victim role, they are most likely to see their partner as the aggressive attacker and themselves as put upon, unfairly accused, mistreated, and unappreciated. The most common emotion they feel is fear, and they most often react with the third horseman of the apocalypse: defensiveness.

If playing the righteous indignation role, their inner thoughts are similar to those in the innocent victim, but also include two additional feelings toward their spouse for trying to victimize them: hostility and contempt. This often leads to desires for revenge and they start to look for ways to inflict pain.

2. *Contempt:* This all-consuming mind-set of negativity usually leads a couple to step two in the cycle of negativity. In this stage, the couple reacts with the first apocalypse horseman, criticism, and then moves on to horsemen two, contempt.

Criticism goes several steps beyond the often-helpful complaint. Instead of attacking the issue or event, they escalate to attacking the person. Instead of speaking in specifics such as, "It was your turn to do the dishes and you watched TV instead," they say things like, "You're not much of a husband these days."

But contempt takes it a step further with revenge-seeking verbal bombs intended to maim and hurt their enemy. Like if they were to say something like, "You didn't do the dishes again! You're a total idiot and the laziest bum on earth." These types of statements are not easily forgotten or forgiven, hence why Gottman labels them apocalyptic, as they are so destructive.

The sad thing about this cycle is that it could and should end before it gets to this point. The person receiving the criticism or even contemptuous remarks always has a choice.

3a and 3b. *Distress maintaining or self-soothing:* The first choice a partner has as a victim to his or her mate's attacks is choosing to think such distress-maintaining thoughts as, *How dare you!* and proceed to escalate the confrontation (step 3b on the "Cycle of Negativity" chart). The second choice they have is choosing to refuse to take offense and self-soothe instead (step 3a).

Attacked mates can choose to view evil communication not as a personal attack but rather as an indication of just how upset their partner is with the situation and how bad of a day he or she is having. If the attacked are humble and truly concerned about the well-being of their mate, they will choose to focus on their partner's feelings and concerns rather than seek prideful revenge and automatically return evil for the evil received.

4. *Defensiveness:* If dating or married couples choose to maintain the distressful negative thought pattern, then they invite increased entropy and the third apocalyptic horseman into their marriages: defensiveness. Each of these four horsemen is more harmful to the relationship than the preceding one.

Defensiveness is more harmful than criticism or contempt because it cuts off helpful dialogue. There can't be any meaningful problem-solving dialogue with someone who refuses to accept any responsibility for his or her behavior. The victimhood act includes constant emotional whining about the unfairness of it all and a refusal to see things in any other way than the one that benefits the offended party.

They often employ "yes-butting," a technique that gives the appearance of listening to the other's reasoning but usually ends with a, "*Yes,* we could try that, *but* it won't work." Or they may use the "rubber-man or rubber-woman" ploy. Whatever they are confronted with is quickly turned around and thrown right back at the complainer: "You think I'm selfish? You should look in a mirror." Again, the listener has trifled with the complaints of his or her partner and refused to acknowledge that he or she has any need to change, acting like he or she isn't the problem.

A final tactic is to act like he or she is listening to the complaint, but then just keep coming back to the same defense logic that preserves "innocence." When someone does this, he or she sends the message that the other's logic and feelings are never going to get through. So the complainer might as well just give up.

At this point, either (or preferably both) of the partners should come to the realization that the argument is going nowhere and go back to the former step where the couple can choose to calm down and listen to understand rather than listen just to develop a winning strategy. If the two can cut off this destructive horseman at this stage, then the damage can be repaired and entropy contained. However, if instead of self-soothing, distress-maintaining is chosen and they escalate the argument, then they go to step five and the fourth apocalyptic horseman, thus going further down the slippery slope.

5. *Stonewall:* To stonewall your partner is to build a figurative stone wall between yourself and him or her on the issue and refuse to talk about it anymore. Basically, someone is being uncooperative, obstructive, or evasive, refusing to comply or cooperate. It is the worst horseman because problems have no chance to be solved or even discussed when partners angrily storms away and locks a door between them and their mate. By mentally freeing themselves of any responsibility for the conflict, they don't have to do any work. None of it is then "their fault."

For a variety of reasons, men stonewall far more than women. However, in the following story, it is the woman who loved to stonewall. The young couple had been married only a few of years and the wife had fallen into a pattern of stomping off to the bedroom and locking the door when she got angry during a discussion—which was most of the time. She would shut herself off from her husband for hours.

The husband finally decided to put an end to this problem, so secretly he reversed the lock on the bedroom door. A few days later during the next heated discussion, the wife predictably tried to perform her disappearing act and angrily ran for the bedroom. The husband followed her, begging her to stay and rationally discuss the problem. She slammed the door in his face and he heard her trying to lock it. The husband quickly locked the door from the outside and announced to her, "And you can stay in the bedroom until you learn to control your temper and be civil!"

It was only a couple minutes before she meekly knocked on the door and asked to be released. He left her in the bedroom for the next four hours. The stonewalling ended, and years later they still laugh about the incident.

If stonewalling occurs, the solution is to self-soothe and be patient. If a couple stubbornly chooses distress-maintaining thoughts instead, then they escalate the argument to step six and accelerate time's arrow onward toward the destruction of the relationship.

6. *Flooding:* If in the angry solitude of a couple's stonewalling they allow the contention and anger to ferment and evolve, then the next predictable behavior is to flood. When flooded, heartbeats accelerate, muscles tighten, and mental systems overload. This state can come about because of more than a reaction to stonewalling, but when it occurs, there is little chance for rational discussion.

When one or both partners in a relationship flood, it is time for a time-out. No one is an innocent victim to his or her emotions, and everyone always has choices. Have you ever seen someone in a heated argument quickly gain composure to answer the phone or door? We can all mentally self-soothe and choose to calm down if we really want to. If partners choose to hold onto the hurt and continue to use their anger to "win" the fight, then they continue to slide down the slippery slope to step seven.

7. *The distance and isolation cascade:* At this stage, four things happen. First, the couples grow even more negative in their mind-sets and start to see problems as severe and unsolvable. Second, their negativity has made it now seem useless to try to talk things out. Third, entropy hardens and they start to drift apart into their own worlds and spend less and less time together. And fourth, loneliness sets in and they become more vulnerable to extramarital affairs.

8. *Rewrite marital history:* In the final stage, the couples' inner scripts become so distorted that they cannot remember the past with any kind of accuracy. They see the past only through the darkly distorted blinders they insist on wearing. These blinders are sunglasses that block out the light of truth and are fashioned from the depth of their constantly fed ultra-negative view of their intimate enemy.

Rejoiceth Not in Iniquity

Orson Pratt said, "A wicked man can have but little love for his wife" ("Celestial Marriage," *The Seer*, October 1853, 156). I've shown my students this quote for years and asked them, "Is Orson Pratt right? Why can't a wicked man show love for his wife?" Nearly all my students agree with Elder Pratt. Most of them explain that wickedness always involves selfishness in one form or another, and selfishness is the opposite of pure love.

I believe my students have it right and that response is a good, all-purpose answer, as is the scripture, "Wickedness never was happiness" (Alma 41:10). Four additional scriptures help understand the negative relationship between wickedness and love:

- "And because iniquity shall abound, the love of many shall wax cold" (Matthew 24:12).
- "And the love of men shall wax cold, and iniquity shall abound" (D&C 45:27). Iniquity and love cannot coexist because iniquity thinks exclusively of itself, whereas love focuses on the needs of others.
- Evilness is ruled by the unfettered natural man lusts of the flesh, whereas for true love to exist there must be discipline and self-mastery. "Also see that ye bridle all your passions, that ye may be filled with love" (Alma 38:12).
- King Benjamin taught, "For the natural man is an enemy to God, and has been from the fall of Adam, and will be, forever and ever, unless he yields to the enticings of the Holy Spirit, and putteth off the natural man" (Mosiah 3:19).

King Benjamin actually was describing Freud's id versus ego and super-ego conflict model long before Freud wrote it. According to Freud's model of the psyche, the "id" is the set of uncoordinated instinc-tual trends, which King Benjamin calls the natural man. Freud's "ego" is the organized, realistic part where mankind is supposed to think of the consequences of their behavior before they act. The "super-ego" plays the critical and moralizing role, or what King Benjamin refers to as the light of Christ conscience we are all born with that guides us to correct decisions.

We live in perilous times where the conscience is under attack and many are trying to extinguish the light of Christ. Paul described this latter-day apostasy from truth and the light of Christ: "Now the Spirit speaketh expressly, that in the latter times some shall depart from the faith, giving heed to seducing spirits, and doctrines of devils; speaking lies in hypocrisy; having their conscience seared with a hot iron" (1 Timothy 4:1–2).

Paul used the comparison of being seared with a hot iron in order to explain what he saw people doing in the last days to their conscience—deadening it to the point where it has no feeling and thus has no effectiveness.

The result today is a world where many of its inhabitants have seared their consciences and are now slaves to their passions and appetites. They have become what Nephi and Mormon referred to as "past feeling": "Thou knowest the wickedness of this people; thou knowest that they are without principle, and past feeling" (Moroni 9:20). "Ye are swift to do iniquity but slow to remember the Lord your God. Ye have seen an angel, and he spake unto you; yea, ye have heard his voice from time to time; and he hath spoken unto you in a still small voice, but ye were past feeling, that ye could not feel his words" (1 Nephi 17:45).

Being past feeling is a state that is deadly to eternal relationships and especially to our ability to maintain them. There are many forms of iniquity that can take us "past feeling," but probably the most damaging today is pornography addiction. In the last ten years of my teaching career, I saw a two-fold increase every year in the number of students coming in for help with their addiction to pornography. Most were returned missionaries trying to regain the Spirit after having been seduced by this evil mistress.

The Church has numerous resources for members struggling with this monster. There is an online site dedicated to helping members overcome pornography addiction that can be reached via lds.org. Priesthood leaders can also direct members to LDS addiction recovery programs.

Second to pornography for effectiveness in killing true love is what I call the apostasy pattern. It starts with a strong temptation in an area in which we are susceptible. This is followed by a gradual loss of enthusiasm for keeping the commandment that pertains to the area, and then gradually there is a loss of enthusiasm for keeping all commandments. Next comes a loss of testimony, followed by inactivity in Church attendance.

Moroni's admonition is to "rejoiceth not in iniquity but rejoiceth in the truth." I've seen the apostasy pattern unfold many times, from Vietnam to America, with people of all ages, not just our youth. They look at the parties going on in the great and spacious building and feel they are missing out on too much fun. They then let go of the iron rod and take the forbidden path to the utterly foundationless building of "good times."

Once the believers have partaken of the debaucheries and the forbidden fruit, they are confronted by their consciences and experience the cognitive dissonance I explained earlier in this book. This conflict between our moral reasoning taught by the light of Christ and our lusts of the flesh cannot go on—"No man can serve two masters: for either he will hate the one, and love the other; or else he will hold to the one, and despise the other. Ye cannot serve God and mammon" (Matthew 6:24).

The easiest choice is to just simply say, "I no longer believe in morality or in the Church that advocates the plan of happiness. I've found a better path to what I think is happiness." We do this because it's far easier to stop believing in something than it is to actually change addictive behaviors.

Inactivity in the Church follows because it is more comfortable for us to associate with people who think and feel the same way we do. When we arrive at this sorry state, we have followed the exact opposite counsel of Moroni to finding true love. We have chosen to rejoice in iniquity and ignore truth, and this choice will never lead to finding eternal happiness.

Summary

This chapter examined the remaining five areas of Moroni's model for achieving pure love. It covers those behaviors to avoid if we want to find, develop, and keep perfect love:

- Envy ("envieth not")
- Pride ("is not puffed up")
- Selfishness ("seeketh not her own")
- Negativity ("thinketh no evil")
- Iniquity ("rejoiceth not in iniquity")

Applying True Love Self-Evaluation Questions—Part 2

Envy

- How do you rate your ability to keep these relationship killers in check: envy, jealousy, greed, covetousness, resentment, and spitefulness?
  - A. I do well most of the time
  - B. Sometimes I let these feelings slip in
  - C. I spend a lot of time fighting these feelings

- Are you ever guilty of borrowing beyond your means because you're envious of those around you who appear to be wealthier?
  - A. Never
  - B. Sometimes
  - C. More than I should

- Do you sincerely rejoice in your partner's or friends' successes? Do you support your partner or friends in their important interests, activities, and callings, celebrating their talents?
  - A. Always
  - B. Usually
  - C. Seldom

- If married, have you always done your best to help your mate feel important, respected, and completely equal in the relationship?
  - A. Always
  - B. Usually
  - C. I've never thought about it; maybe I should

Pride

- In spirited discussions with your mate or friends, do you keep behaviors in check that could be interpreted as self-centered, boastful, arrogant, or haughty?
  A. Always
  B. Usually
  C. Seldom

- Do you ever get so upset that you think, *Nobody is going to tell me what to do*, or something along those lines?
  A. Never
  B. Sometimes
  C. More than I should

- When discussing a subject where you and your mate or friends have a substantial difference of opinion, do you consistently (and humbly) try to seek a celestial state of cooperation and collaboration?
  A. Always
  B. Usually
  C. Seldom

- When you can't reach celestial cooperation and collaboration, are you at least able to reach a terrestrial level of compromise?
  A. Always
  B. Usually
  C. Seldom

- In your problem-solving discussions, do you stubbornly stick to your telestial guns and try to defeat your companion in what could be seen as a form of marital-mortal combat?
  A. Seldom, if ever
  B. Sometimes
  C. More often than I should

- Have you allowed your desires, appetites, and passions to go unbridled?
  A. Hardly ever
  B. Sometimes
  C. More often than I should

- Does your mate or do your friends think you are stubbornly independent?
  A. Probably not
  B. Maybe a little
  C. I don't know

- How often are you guilty of "pride from the bottom looking up"?
  A. Seldom, if ever
  B. Sometimes
  C. More often than I should

- You never use temper tantrums and anger to get your way and make sure no one ever rules over you.
  A. True
  B. Mostly true
  C. False

- Do you seek to avoid unrighteous dominion, abuse, criticism, contempt, defensiveness, and stonewalling?
  A. Always
  B. Usually
  C. Seldom

Selfishness

- Are you willing to commit to making unselfish sacrifices that are necessary for an eternal marriage?
  A. Absolutely
  B. The majority of the time
  C. I'm not ready for that yet

- Are you willing to put aside your personal comforts, interests, and desires for the good of a family?
  A. Absolutely
  B. The majority of the time
  C. I'm not ready for that yet
  D. I'm tired of doing that all these years

- Are you willing to put aside your personal comforts, interests, and desires for a relationship?
  A. Absolutely
  B. The majority of the time
  C. I'm not ready for that yet

- Do any of the following describe you and your values: personal happiness first and foremost, individual and personal freedom, liberation, adult-centered, career-centered, personal growth-oriented, self-fulfillment first, self-gratification, self-seeking, or self-centered?
  A. Not really
  B. Sometimes
  C. Usually

- Do you work hard to keep your thoughts positive about your eternal companion?
  A. Nearly always
  B. Usually
  C. Hardly ever any more

- You rarely stoop to criticism.
  A. True
  B. Mostly true
  C. False, as I am often critical of the behavior of others

- You rarely use contempt in interactions.
  A. True
  B. Mostly true
  C. False, as I am guilty of it

- You choose not be defensive or take offense when your spouse or friend is expressing a complaint.
  A. True
  B. Mostly true
  C. False, as I often feel that way and act accordingly

- You hang in there during discussions and would never stonewall anyone.
  A. Always
  B. Usually
  C. It's a habit now; I have to get out of there when he or she expresses complaints

- If you become angry or upset during an argument, you know how to call a time-out and get back under control.
  A. Yes, I do
  B. Usually
  C. No, I stay out of control for a while

Iniquity

- Do you try to live a righteous life, and is it a part of your value system?
  A. Yes, and if I slip up, I quickly try to repent
  B. I try but there are a few things I won't let go of yet
  C. I don't even try anymore
- Are you able to keep the apostasy pattern away from yourself?
  A. Always
  B. Sometimes I'm tempted, but I'm still active
  C. It's creeping up on me and it's getting hard to hold off
  D. It's got me

Chapter 9: Compassion

Successful marriages and families are established and maintained by consistently applying the principle of compassion.

Understanding the Compassion Principle

Compassion is the byproduct of learning how to apply the correct principles of faith, prayer, forgiveness, respect, and love while developing the ability to keep natural man pride in check. A compassionate person is keenly aware of the needs of others and naturally wants to help them.

Compassion is the capacity to feel another person's unhappiness or misfortune. The opposite of compassion includes such way-off-from-true-love feelings as callousness, coldheartedness, hard-heartedness, and heartlessness. Near antonyms include such love-killing attitudes as indifference, insensitivity, unconcern, cruelty, harshness, inhumanity, animosity, antipathy, dislike, hatred, and hostility. Selfishness is also a major killer of compassion.

Pride Versus Compassion

In chapter seven, we examined the relationship between pride and respect: The "origin of the majority of all serious forms of relationship-destroying behaviors . . . comes from pride in one form or another." I explained the beginnings and further development of pride. First, we become famous in our own eyes. Then this pride causes us to have feelings of entitlement where we think rules, laws, commandments, and principles simply don't apply to us anymore. Next, those feelings of entitlement lead to attitudes of competition and disrespect for both those we see as above us and those we see as below us. And finally, we treat both those above us and below us with contempt as we trifle with their words and feelings and are plain mean to most everyone around us.

Pride is therefore presented as the number one contender for the title of compassion killer in this book. This logic can also be reversed: The number one contender for the title of pride killer is compassion. Pride and compassion are incompatible—they cannot coexist anymore than we can serve God and mammon at the same time. If you are motivated to put pride in its proper place (which is hell), then work on increasing your capacity for compassion.

Love and Compassion

We could label compassion as a subcategory of *agape*-type love and just include the topic in the love chapters, but that's not the way it is presented in paragraph seven of "The Family: A Proclamation to the World." The Church leadership list it separately, just after love in the presentation order of the nine principles upon which "successful marriages and families are established and maintained." This should tell us that compassion is important by itself.

In chapter eight, we learned that love is a multifaceted topic. There is *eros*, the erotic physical side of love; *philos*, the deep friendship type of love; and *agape*, the altruistic and non-demanding part of love. Compassion is similar to *agape* love but seems to take it a step further and emphasize the importance of alertly noticing and responding to a partner's needs, especially in times of crisis.

If we truly love our mates, we show consistent compassion for them by being sensitive to both their minor daily stresses and also their larger problems. It is then vitally important that we get up and actually do something about these needs whenever possible.

The importance of compassion in marriage is underscored in one of President Hinckley's statements, quoted also in chapter eight: "I am satisfied that happiness in marriage is not so much a matter of romance [*eros*] as it is an anxious concern for the comfort and well-being of one's companion [*agape* and pure compassion]."[56]

Examples of Compassion

The Savior gave us many examples of pure compassion. Jesus saw people's needs, was moved with compassion for them, and then did something about it:

- "And Jesus went about all the cities and villages, teaching in their synagogues, and preaching the gospel of the kingdom, and healing every sickness and every disease among the people. But when he saw the multitudes, he was moved with compassion on them, because they fainted, and were scattered abroad, as sheep having no shepherd" (Matthew 9:35–36).
- "And Jesus went forth, and saw a great multitude, and was moved with compassion toward them, and he healed their sick" (Matthew 14:14).
- "So Jesus had compassion on them, and touched their eyes: and immediately their eyes received sight, and they followed him" (Matthew 20:33–34).
- "And Jesus, moved with compassion, put forth his hand, and touched him, and saith unto him, I will; be thou clean" (Mark 1:41).
- "In those days the multitude being very great, and having nothing to eat, Jesus called his disciples unto him, and saith unto them, I have compassion on the multitude, because they have now been with me three days, and have nothing to eat" (Mark 8:1–2).
- "And he asked them, How many loaves have ye? And they said, Seven. And he commanded the people to sit down on the ground: and he took the seven loaves, and gave thanks, and brake, and gave to his disciples to set before them; and they did set them before the people. And they had a few small fishes: and he blessed, and commanded to set them also before them" (Mark 8:4–7).

- "And when the Lord saw her, he had compassion on her, and said unto her, Weep not. And he came and touched the bier: and they that bare him stood still. And he said, Young man, I say unto thee, Arise" (Luke 7:12–14).

We may not have the capacity to multiply loaves of bread and fish and feed the masses, nor always be able to heal the sick or alleviate the sorrow of a widowed mother by bringing her child back from the dead, but there is much we can do in times of great need that can come close to equaling these great miracles.

Examples of Compassion During Extreme Hardships

Life sometimes throws adversity at us, a fair amount of the time through no fault of our own. It just seems to be the random nature of the world we live in, or possibly we, seeking greater blessings, volunteered for hazardous duty in our premortal existence. I don't know of any one specific principle that explains why tragedy strikes some families and passes over others.

I have watched friends drop all of their remaining life goals to care for their stricken eternal mate in his or her time of need. Again, I have no idea why some are stricken with such debilitating problems as Alzheimer's disease, dementia, multiple sclerosis, cancer, Parkinson's disease, diabetes, freak accidents resulting in paralysis, and so on, and yet all the while others are not. But as I watch my friends heroically take care of their mates, there is one thing I'm certain of: they are well on their way to earning their exaltation based on these compassionate acts alone.

I can recall an acquaintance years ago whose wife of only a few months tragically became a quadriplegic in an automobile accident. She needed total care and couldn't even talk to say thank you. She could only communicate through her eyes. This courageous and compassionate man adapted his life to be able to care for her. He took her to church, to the movies, and to other places on a gurney where she could listen and watch using a mirror he set up for her. He sacrificed everything for her and received little reward in return. He had done this for over twenty years when I first met him years ago. I suspect his compassion is near perfect.

All of my friends in these situations chose to care for their eternal mate because they first had a solid foundation of the principles of faith, prayer, forgiveness, respect, and love to work off of. I think their prowess in these principles gave them the strength to perform these seemingly impossible compassionate tasks. As a result of performing their compassionate service, their capacity to give and receive faith, prayer, forgiveness, respect, and love increased. It appears that the development of any one of these perfecting principles increases all the others and speeds the compassionate person rapidly forward toward exaltation.

Another extremely difficult stressor that many couples need to deal with using the compassion principle is handicapped or special needs children. Many valiant parents have compassionately taken care of the needs of these children for years and years. I watched my own parents deal with the needs of a severely handicapped Down syndrome child for over forty years. Their capacity for compassion grew proportionally with the many needs of this child. They endured to the end and were different and far better people from having had the experience.

I often contrast my parents' experience with my Down syndrome sister to that of a middle-aged woman I met in Australia in 1964 while serving my mission. She invited my companion and me in and quickly shared how miserable her life was because she was required to care for her Down syndrome child. She was truly depressed and no longer saw a purpose to her life. I marveled at the difference in attitude and quality of life between that woman and my parents. The difference was that one couple saw compassionate service as an opportunity and embraced it enthusiastically while the other lacked the compassion to see any kind of silver lining in the clouds and chose to be miserable.

Paul Explained Tribulation and the Need for Compassion

Paul, in his Epistle to the Romans, explained how the principles covered in this book can strengthen each other and ultimately us when adversity hits: "And not only so, but we glory in tribulations also: knowing that tribulation worketh patience; And patience, experience; and experience, hope: And hope maketh not ashamed; because the love of God is shed abroad in our hearts by the Holy Ghost which is given unto us" (Romans 5:3–5).

Here is my interpretation of Paul's teachings: Paul explained that, when endured well, life's tribulations can increase our patience. The importance of patience has been discussed in several of the preceding chapters. It keeps coming up for good reason. Without patience, we cannot perfect any of the principles necessary for a love that lasts for all eternity.

Paul taught that patience leads to experience. To have these experiences is why we all voted in the premortal existence to come to this earth and take our chances. By facing enough tribulations and difficult challenges, we gain patience and become tribulation veterans. Along the way, we also learn how to deal with many types of adversity as they come our way.

Successfully defeating adversity leads us to hope, and then it's onto a powerful faith that we can overcome even more adversity if called upon to do so. This hope that leads us to faith should dissipate any feelings of shame or embarrassment we have as a result of what others might think of our tribulation experiences. Paul concluded by telling us that it is the Holy Ghost that brings these peaceful insights to our minds and ultimately gives us the strength to endure and win in the end.

Examples of Compassion in Moderate and Minor Hardships

Eventually, there is need for compassion in all marriages, whether it is because of catastrophic physical health issues or less disruptive tribulations sometimes caused by our own actions. Here are a few true-life examples of relationship problems where either the husband or the wife (or both) needed to apply the principle of compassion for their love and marriage to endure in happiness:

- A young husband experiences erectile dysfunction early in their marriage. His new wife is frustrated but wants to know what she can do to help.
- A new husband learns soon after the wedding that his wife was sexually abused when she was a child and is fearful of intercourse. The husband wants to know how to best help her.

- A husband expresses feelings of frustration to his wife concerning the frequency of and quality of their sexual intimacy. She ponders how to respond as she feels they are intimate too often and is not comfortable with all of his desires during their sexual experiences.
- A wife desperately desires to become a mother but seems unable to get pregnant.
- A couple has children. The mother devotes her life to rearing them in righteousness and prepares them for success in the world. She wakes up one day to find her home an empty nest as all the children have moved out into the world. She now struggles to find meaning to her life.
- A husband loses his job and struggles to find new employment that will pay the bills.
- A wife becomes addicted to painkillers.
- A husband fights his pornography addiction.
- A faithful bishop's wife tells her husband she no longer believes the Church is true and she will no longer be active in it. How should the bishop react? What are his options?
- A once-faithful returned missionary husband and father tells his wife after fifteen years of marriage he is asking that his name be removed from the Church records. He does not want their children to be baptized or even attend church.
- An active LDS couple learns their returned missionary son is homosexual and is living with his new partner.
- A young couple listen to the missionary lessons. The wife and children accept baptism; the husband gives his permission for her and the children to do so, but he will not be baptized. She lives the next twenty-five years of her life in a part-member family, wishing she could have a temple marriage and have her children sealed to them. She now wonders if she made a mistake staying with her husband all those years and thus contemplates leaving him.
- A husband fights weakly to control his weight as he approaches four hundred pounds. It bothers his wife greatly.

In each one of these *real* situations, the partner being asked to be patient with his or her spouse's problem was able to apply the principle of compassion and chose to stay in love, help his or her mate, and remain married. Several of them learned that compassion is far more powerful than prideful reactions that lead to contention and nagging and marital disfunction.

The erectile dysfunction couple required several years to find the right medical solution that finally helped them out. The wife's patient compassion saved her marriage. The wife who was sexually abused as a child was able to adjust more quickly to marriage thanks to the compassionate understanding of her husband. The couple with differing sexual expectations was able to reach a compromise because each sincerely wanted their spouse to be happy, so they continued to communicate about it until the problem was solved. The infertile wife, with the compassionate sympathy of her husband, eventually accepted her plight and she and her husband are now enjoying their adopted children. The couple with the son who had feelings of same-sex attraction continued to love him and didn't allow the situation to drive the family apart, even though he aggressively tested their patience by making unreasonable demands that he knew would embarrass them.

Some of these Saints will have to wait until they reach the other side of the veil for the final solution to their trials. However, the compassion they choose to give others in their experiences will certainly weigh favorably in the balance at their final judgment.

No one will be denied exaltation in the end because he or she stayed the course and compassionately attempted to help his or her spouse or children wake up and partake of the precious fruit found on the tree of life. In the end, exaltation will not be denied those who sought it diligently all their lives and—often through no fault of their own—could not live perfectly the law upon which that blessing is predicated.

If our attitudes and intentions are pure, we know "that it is by grace that we are saved, after all we can do" (2 Nephi 25:23).

Disclaimer

However, there are times in intimate relationships when our being compassionate is not the right answer. If one of the partners is physically, sexually, spiritually, or emotionally abusive of the other, compassion does not require patiently and stoically accepting this great evil. We all have agency, and there are times when the right thing to do is to choose to take the steps necessary to get help and stop the problem. Sister Aileen H. Clyde gives the following insight in the October 1991 general conference:

> If charity is not always quick to our understanding, it may occasionally be quick to our misunderstanding. It is not charity or kindness to endure any type of abuse or unrighteousness that may be inflicted on us by others. God's commandment that as we love him we must respect ourselves suggests we must not accept disrespect from others. It is not charity to let another repeatedly deny our divine nature and agency. It is not charity to bow down in despair and helplessness. That kind of suffering should be ended, and that is very difficult to do alone. There are priesthood leaders and other loving servants who will give aid and strength when they *know* of the need. We must be willing to let others help us.[57]

I can recall two different counseling cases illustrating Sister Clyde's point. The first was years ago, involving a young woman who professed to no longer believe in any religion. She came to counseling because she was depressed, lonely, and angry with herself and had extremely low self-esteem because her husband had recently filed for divorce. She told of an incident on her husband's birthday when he suggested that they participate in "open marriage" sexual activities. It was not something she wanted to do but decided to go along with his request because it was his birthday.

As they continued to participate in these activities over the next few months, she noticed her husband's behavior toward her change. Where he used to be kind and considerate toward her, he was now rude, impatient, critical, and short-tempered. Respect for her was gone and along with it the marriage, leaving her to ignorantly wondering what happened to her marriage and her life.

A second case involved a young Latter-day Saint wife with a strong testimony and an inactive husband. On New Year's Eve, her husband invited another couple over and, later that night, her husband and the other couple suggested the same open marriage–type activity as the first couple described above.

This young woman, with righteous indignation, refused and held her moral high ground and demanded the other couple immediately leave or she would call the police. Her iron will prevailed and her husband meekly spent the next several nights on the couch. At his wife's insistence (ultimatum), they met with their bishop, who helped them get their marriage back on track with prevailing gospel standards. It's never compassionate to agree to lower your standards in order to please someone who suggests evil.

Compassion's Place in the Plan of Salvation

Jesus revealed a radical new doctrine to His disciples in John 13:34: "A new commandment I give unto you, That ye love one another; as I have loved you, that ye also love one another." The old law that the disciples were familiar with was one of strict observance of orthodox commandments right down to how many steps a person could walk on the Sabbath. Not that strict obedience is a bad thing, but history shows that radical observance of religion devoid of compassion is a recipe for disaster. We need look no further than the events of 9/11 for an example of that.

Jesus brought compassion to the forefront of religious observation. He appears to have made it the heart and core of discipleship: "By this shall all men know that ye are my disciples, if ye have love one to another" (John 13:35).

How exactly do we show this love? John answered that in 1 John 3:17–18: "But whoso hath this world's good, and seeth his brother have need, and shutteth up his bowels of compassion from him, how dwelleth the love of God in him? My little children, let us not love in word, neither in tongue; but in deed and in truth." The essence of following the Savior is to do as He did. First, we notice a brother in need and have compassion for him. Second, we do not simply talk about his problems. Instead, if we have the resources to do so, use those resources to alleviate his needs.

Needs and Wants

If compassion is being aware of and trying to alleviate the needs of others, then we could ask the question, "Is this a real need?" In the scriptures, needs and wants are discussed three different times. The first two seem to imply that both are equally important.

- "And this he said unto them, having been commanded of God; and they did walk uprightly before God, imparting to one another both temporally and spiritually according to their needs and their wants" (Mosiah 18:29).
- "Wherefore, let my servant Edward Partridge . . . appoint unto this people their portions, every man equal according to his family, according to his circumstances and his wants and needs" (D&C 51:3).

The third scripture, also dealing with the administration of the united order, suggests that it may be prudent to determine if a person's wants are justified or not.

- "And you are to be equal, or in other words, you are to have equal claims on the properties, for the benefit of managing the concerns of your stewardships, every man according to his wants and his needs, inasmuch as his wants are just" (D&C 82:17).

It is possible—and even probable—that a spouse could sometimes abuse the compassionate nature of his or her mate and try to manipulate for personal gain. This is not a strategy that will last long-term, as compassion will eventually be replaced with resentment in the victim. It's also a gross violation of the compassion principle to manipulate another in this manner. However, the first two scriptures appear to teach that a person's wants are important. We all have a basic need to be appreciated and valued. When we go out of our way to alleviate the wants of our loved ones as well as their needs, then we are closing in on eternal love with greater accuracy and the compassion we give is often returned two-fold.

The things that men and women want after their basic needs are met may seem a little strange and even downright bizarre to those of the opposite sex. I have heard many women comment on how ridiculous men look dressed in leather as they ride their motorcycles around the country. Yet some of these same women will buy those leather riding outfits for their men for Christmas or birthdays just to see them happy.

Many of those same men view things like expensive hair products, name brand clothing, pedicures, manicures, eyelash extensions, facial products, thirty pairs of shoes, and multiple purses as a total waste of money but will provide them because they compassionately want to make their wives happy. Individual perspectives on the *what* don't matter so much when we focus on the *who*.

Compassion often comes into play when each of our wants exceed our budget and there is competition for scarce resources in trying to obtain our wants. Pure love requires that we think of each other's needs and wants first and then strive for a fair balance.

The Ideal: It Is Not Good to Be Alone

Overcoming tribulations is often a hard thing to do by ourselves. Besides the comfort gained through faith and effective prayer, it is often the compassionate service of others in these times of need that gives us the final strength to carry on through and defeat the tribulation. This is yet another reason why it is "not good to be alone" (Genesis 2:18) in this mortal existence of seemingly random tribulations and frail existence.

The great plan of happiness teaches us the ideal for which we ought to strive. First, we are born of goodly parents, whose compassionate service prepares us to be married and to create our own eternal family unit when we have grown and learned. In marriage, we commit to compassionately take care of one another and the new family that will be made together. Finally, in our old age, our children are often given the opportunity to grow spiritually by giving us the compassionate service we need to endure in dignity unto the end of our mortal days. Compassion, at every stage of our lives, is at the heart of the plan of salvation, or the great plan of happiness (Alma 42:8). Compassion kills all forms of pride and helps to keep eternal family units together forever.

Compassion is the means by which we live the first and second great commandments. The first commandment is, "Thou shalt love the Lord thy God with all thy heart, and with all thy soul, and with all thy mind. This is the first and great commandment" (Matthew 22:37–38). We can't fully love the Lord unless we fulfill the first requirement of compassion, which is to recognize His needs. God's greatest work and glory and need is "to bring to pass the immortality and eternal life of man" (Moses 1:39).

Once we are aware of our obligation to assist God in His great work, we then need to get busy and fulfill the second requirement of compassion: to alleviate needs as best we can. We do that by keeping the second great commandment, "And the second is like unto it, Thou shalt love thy neighbour as thyself" (Matthew 22:39).

The "neighbors" closest to you should always be your companions and family. If you're not in an intimate relationship, you still have many opportunities in your daily life to keep pride and selfishness in check through compassionate service within the community in which you live.

To use the compassion principle doesn't always require gigantic sacrifices. Sometimes it's just being aware of each other's needs and doing something about it. One young lady shared this story of her husband's compassion:

> Sometimes my husband knows what I need more than even I do. With working two jobs, finals, and projects coming up and the stress of transferring and moving soon, I'd been getting little sleep and more stressed by the day.
>
> A few days ago, I had a rare day off but planned on rising early to get a good start on several projects, and I asked him to wake me at six or seven (he was up early that day).
>
> The next morning, I woke with horror to see noon on the clock! I burst out of our room, explaining that I overslept to find the dishes done, the house clean, and Zach sitting on the couch. He told me that he had turned off our alarm clock before it woke me and snuck out early. He said he could tell how much I needed a good sleep, so instead he took care of the chores to allow me the time I needed for my projects that afternoon.
>
> What a sweetheart! My eyes filled with tears and my love for him grew all the more. He is a darling example of selfless sacrifice and compassion, and I do my absolute best to do the same for him and all those around me.

Summary

Compassion has two parts: a sympathetic awareness of the distresses of others and a desire to alleviate those distresses. We should strive to alleviate both the needs and the wants of others when possible. Compassion is the natural byproduct of learning to apply the correct principles of faith, prayer, forgiveness, respect, and love.

Increasing compassionate behaviors is the prescription for such love-killing and relationship-ending behaviors as indifference, insensitivity, unconcern, cruelty, harshness, animosity, antipathy, dislike, hatred, hostility, and good old-fashioned selfishness. Compassion for others is also one of the best antidotes for the universal detonator of all things sinful: pride.

Examples of compassion were presented from the Savior's life, from student's lives, and from counseling settings. The point was made that we may not always have the ability to perform a miracle to relieve the suffering of a loved one, but we can be perfect in our compassionate desire to do so and in our efforts to try. It was also pointed out that being compassionate to someone who is intent on abusing us is neither charitable nor appropriate. In conclusion, we noted compassion, in the plan of salvation, is at or near the heart of the great plan of happiness and the fulfillment of the first and second great commandments given in Matthew 22.

Applying Compassion Self-Evaluation Questions

- How sensitive are you to the needs of those you are close to, be it your spouse, family, or friends?
  A. I think I'm aware of the majority of their needs
  B. Some of their needs slip by me from time to time
  C. They are a mystery to me most of the time
  D. I rarely ever notice the needs of those around me

- How do you think those you're close to would rate your awareness of their needs?
  A. High
  B. Average
  C. Needs improvement

- When you are aware of other's needs, how often do you try your best to help?
  A. 100%
  B. 75–100%
  C. 50–75%
  D. Less than 50%

Chapter 10: Work

Successful marriages and families are established and maintained by consistently applying the principle of work.

Understanding the Work Principle

The origin of man's need to work occurred because of an incident in the Garden of Eden. The result was this: "Thou shalt not eat of it: cursed is the ground for thy sake; in sorrow shalt thou eat of it all the days of thy life; thorns also and thistles shall it bring forth to thee; and thou shalt eat the herb of the field; in the sweat of thy face shalt thou eat bread, till thou return unto the ground; for out of it wast thou taken: for dust thou art, and unto dust shalt thou return" (Genesis 3:17–19).

The short version is, "We are most likely going to work hard all our lives and then we die." To go into an intimate relationship or marriage and think there is no "exertion or labor" expected for keeping it happy and healthy is a little naïve. Relationships are like gardens. If you expect to harvest good results, you have to take the time to work the soil. It will not automatically produce a great harvest. It must be watered, weeded, and prayed over with diligence.

The Book of Mormon puts it this way: "And now behold, if ye nourish it with much care it will get root, and grow up, and bring forth fruit. But if ye neglect the tree, and take no thought for its nourishment, behold it will not get any root; and when the heat of the sun cometh and scorcheth it, because it hath no root it withers away, and ye pluck it up and cast it out" (Alma 32:37–38).

The tree referred to above is one of faith. This is similar to chapter three's presentation of the similarities between the developments of faith in Alma 32 and how eternal love blossoms and reaches maturity. Just as faith takes hard work and diligence to develop and maintain, so does love that's expected to last through eternity.

Examples of Work in Relationships

I've watched the effects of our modern women's movement on the dating, courtship, and marriage stages of life since the 1970s. One result is some modern men feel liberated from traditional gender roles and responsibilities. This creates problems in developing true love in a variety of ways.

In my "Preparing for an Eternal Marriage" classes, I often encouraged the young men to take the initiative and ask young women out on dates. Each week, the students reported on their dating experiences so they could learn from each other.

I recall one handsome recently returned missionary reporting each week on his dating experiences. They all had one thing in common— the girl had taken the initiative to ask him out. He went the entire semester without ever asking a girl on a date, and yet he dated nearly every week. It reminded me of the signs in Yellowstone asking travelers not to feed the bears.

I saw the young man often at the institute for the next three years and sometimes asked him how his love life was going and if he had asked anyone out yet. The answer was always the same: he was having a good time, going on lots of dates and still had not asked anyone out. He graduated single and I have not seen him since. Perhaps we should have put a sign up at the institute, stating, "Do not feed the boys."

I contrast this young man to another who was motivated to follow the prophets' counsel and find an eternal mate as soon as practical upon returning from his mission. He enrolled at BYU and took the initiative, setting a goal to date every week even though he only had a budget of two dollars a week for it. After asking out many different women, he found one that appreciated his particular talents and potential. He liked her also, and they moved the relationship to the courtship stage and in less than a year they were engaged.

I mention that the young woman saw this young man's potential even though all throughout the dating stage he only had two dollars a week to spend on her, so their dates were always simple. She saw that he was a good student, hungry for success, and had a great work ethic and the potential to someday be a good provider. She wanted what most women still want—a husband who's willing to work and get a family-wage job.

Before he met his true love, this young man had several strange dating experiences. He asked one young lady out on a date and she looked at him and asked, "What kind of a car do you drive?" He responded that his uncle had given him a twenty-year-old Peugeot that barely ran, but it had leather seats and a sunroof. She said, "I'm sorry, I only date BMWs." He thought she was kidding until he saw her in town riding with a boy in a new BMW.

I've told this story to my dating classes over the years and asked, "What's the matter with the kind of thinking that concludes, *I'm only going to date young men in college that have lots of money and drive nice German cars?*" The answer that comes back from my students is consistent: "There's a high chance that a college boy with lots of money and a fancy car has had everything given to him and an even better chance that he doesn't know how to work. A young man who isn't hungry, motivated, or knows how to work will eventually run out of his parents' money, and then what?"

Nationally, there are dating services dedicated to women who are looking for "a nice guy with a job." To me, this should be obvious, but apparently it's not in our modern liberated world. In one online dating forum, several forum members asked, "Why do guys with jobs attract women?" One young man answered and posted his own question (the following punctuation and spelling is left unedited): "Something strange happens when I find work… I actually attract girls.i cant explain it though becuz i dont tell them that i have a job.. but they magically get attracted to me.. why is that so? can anyone explain this?"

An answer for the young man's question: It is more than just the income men should bring to a relationship, marriage, and family. Men need to work. Our bodies are designed for work. When we refuse to work while we're capable, it affects more than needed income in a relationship—it affects our physical and mental health, our dignity, and our feelings of self-worth. I believe that women can instinctively ("magically") sense all of this.

Until the earth is "renewed and receives its paradisiacal glory," young men and women should look for an eternal mate who knows how to work. However, even then, there is a good chance we will still need to know how to set goals and keep projects on time.

The Principle of Work for Men

Many years ago, a middle-aged man whom I was acquainted with asked for help with his marriage. He seemed panicked and anxious to get things straightened out with his wife of five years. His wife was agreeable to counseling, and we met. It didn't take long to find the source of the contention—he had not had employment since they married five years earlier and his wife was tired of supporting him and listening to his excuses for not working. This was her first marriage and his third.

For several weeks, I listened as he rationalized and made excuses again and again. He claimed his training and professional experience were in a field that technology had made nearly obsolete. He refused to take a job below his dignity and reported former pay scales. It appeared to me he had become comfortable with allowing his wife to bring in all the income and was resistive to finding any kind of job. He couldn't claim to be needed at home taking care of the children because they had none.

Making a long story short, the marriage failed because he refused to work. His wife would have remained married to him if he had just gotten up every day and gone to work at, say, McDonald's. The last time that I saw him, he was literally living in an old van down by the river.

This frustrated woman is far from alone in her feelings these days. Though many men in the world have accepted the new standard of a lesser need to work, Latter-day Saints should know better. Faithful LDS women understand the roles and duties of men and expect them to meet that standard.

The family proclamation explains clearly the work standard for men in paragraph six: "Parents have a sacred duty to rear their children in love and righteousness, *to provide for their physical* and spiritual needs" ("The Family: A Proclamation to the World," *Ensign*, November 1995, 102; emphasis added). Paragraph seven then states, "By divine design, fathers are to preside over their families in love and righteousness and are responsible *to provide the necessities of life* and protection for their families" (emphasis added).

According the family proclamation, men have three primary duties within their roles as husbands and fathers: to preside, protect and provide. These duties are set forth as an important part of the great plan of happiness, and when we try to change them to suit our own fancies, the results are never good.

The family proclamation lists exceptions to this standard, but the intent is certainly not for the exceptions to *become* a new standard: "Mothers are primarily responsible for the nurture of their children. In these sacred responsibilities, fathers and mothers are obligated to help one another as equal partners. Disability, death, or other circumstances may necessitate individual adaptation. Extended families should lend support when needed."

The reasons for these gender responsibilities used to be and still should be clear to the entire world. However, somehow the most basic rules for the survival of the human race are now seen by many as being outdated and are being thrown out, seen as unnecessary, or even as being undesirable. The family proclamation's final two paragraphs clearly warn the world what the result of this foolishness will be: "Further, we warn that the disintegration of the family will bring upon individuals, communities, and nations the calamities foretold by ancient and modern prophets."

The Principle of Work for Women

The gospel standard is simple and clear for men. Men have four roles in the plan of salvation: son, husband, father (or patriarch), and priesthood bearer. Each of these roles comes with multiple responsibilities, duties, and expectations. The three expectations mentioned in the family proclamation of the husband and father roles are to preside, provide, and protect. That's what real priesthood men do. To accomplish these tasks, they are given three gifts: the guidance of the Spirit, upper body strength, and testosterone. The first gift is scripturally verified and the second and third gifts are not doctrinal—just my observations.

Women are a little more complicated. What exactly is the work of a Latter-day Saint woman? Wiser people than I, mostly women, have written a great deal on this topic. We have entire conferences dedicated to the question. I'll try to keep it simple: Like men, women have four analogous roles in the plan of salvation: daughter, wife, mother (or matriarch), and sisterhood. Within the mother (or matriarch) roles, there is only one duty mentioned in the family proclamation: "Mothers are primarily responsible for the nurture of their children."

I often ask my students, "Does that mean that's all women have the talent to do?" After my female students finish throwing things at me, they all agree that's certainly not the case. I then ask how many gifts does it take to accomplish this singular, difficult, and civilization-saving task? They correctly respond that it requires far more than the three gifts men have.

My students have mentioned such gifts as being led by the Spirit; women's intuition; mother's intuition (the ability to know what happens behind closed doors and such); the gifts of compassion, social awareness, and nurturing; being able to use both sides of the brain at the same time; multitasking; the ability to learn new and needed skills; extreme endurance; incredible faith; vast compassion; infinite patience; personal revelation; and the ability to ask for and receive miracles for their families.

When I think of all the skills needed to nurture a child, the closest example I'm aware of is what my wife—the mother of our eight children—had to learn to do her part to get each child ready to leave the nest and succeed in the world. In contrast to do my responsibilities of presiding, protecting, and providing, I spent a lifetime developing just four vocational skills as a teacher, counselor, Army officer, and part-time writer. My wife, during the same time period and out of necessity and our limited resources, gained on-the-job experience and proficiency in many diverse skills. Just a partial list of her child-rearing skills and jobs includes:

- Shuttle bus driver (full-size extended vans)
- EMT (we had six boys)
- Nurse
- Pediatrician
- Consultant
- Gourmet chef
- Short-order cook
- Nutritionist
- Organic gardener
- Home storage keeper
- Storyteller
- Entertainer
- Motivator
- Mediator
- Paper route manager
- Music director
- Sanitation engineer
- Small appliance repair person
- Architect
- Kitchen designer
- Carpenter
- Painter
- Cleaning crew supervisor
- Accountant
- Seamstress
- Barber and beautician
- Bargain hunter and shrewd shopper
- Hostess
- Event planner
- Interior decorator
- Veterinarian
- Zoo keeper
- Dance teacher
- Piano teacher
- Child psychologist
- Coach
- Sports and dance videographer

- Cub scout leader
- Teacher's aide
- Truant officer
- Private investigator
- Project adviser
- Family historian
- Math and science tutor
- English editor
- Driver's education teacher

You get the idea. And to think someone once asked me if my wife worked.

In my marriage classes, after the students have compiled a similar list of gifts and skills it takes to perform the mother role in a family, I ask them, "What else can a woman with these gifts and skill sets do besides nurture their children?" The answer is always the same: "Nearly anything."

Women Working Outside the Home and the Law of Witnesses

Because a good mother has to be proficient at many different roles, the temptation is always present to take those skills and increase the family standard of living by working outside the home. Often, it seems to be the modern, liberated husband who suggests that his wife work outside the home.

The Church's counsel on mothers working outside the home has been consistent over the years. President Spencer W. Kimball, Church president and prophet from December 1973 to November 1985, was the first prophet to have to address the issue. Though women started entering the workforce during World War II, the percentage of LDS mothers working outside the home wasn't incredibly significant until President Kimball's administration.

Succeeding prophets Ezra Taft Benson, Howard W. Hunter, and Gordon B. Hinckley all gave similar counsel to mothers with children still in the home. Elder Henry B. Eyring, then a member of the Quorum of the Twelve Apostles, taught that when a prophet quotes preceding prophets, they are invoking the law of witnesses:

> In our own time we have been warned with counsel on where to find safety from sin and from sorrow. One of the keys to recognizing those

warnings is that they are repeated. For instance, more than once in general conferences, you have heard our prophet say that he would quote a preceding prophet and would therefore be a second witness and sometimes even a third. Each of us old enough to listen heard President Spencer W. Kimball (1895–1985) give counsel on the importance of a mother in the home and then heard President Ezra Taft Benson (1899–1994) quote him, and we have heard President Gordon B. Hinckley (1910–2008) quote them both. The Apostle Paul wrote, "In the mouth of two or three witnesses shall every word be established" (2 Corinthians 13:1). One of the ways we may know that the warning is from the Lord is that the law of witnesses, authorized witnesses, has been invoked. When the words of prophets seem repetitive, that should rivet our attention and fill our hearts with gratitude to live in such a blessed time.[58]

The following are samplings of this law of witnesses counsel given since 1973. I include a somewhat lengthy section of quotes on this topic to allow the reader to feel the full weight of prophetic counsel and warnings on this topic over the years. The complete quotes can be found in the Seminaries and Institutes of Religion publication *Eternal Marriage Student Manual*, 237–240. This and all other institute manuals can be found online at institutes.lds.org.

President Spencer W. Kimball

The husband is expected to support his family and only in an emergency should a wife secure outside employment.

Numerous divorces can be traced directly to the day when the wife left the home and went out into the world into employment. Two incomes raise the standard of living beyond its norm. Two spouses working prevent the complete and proper home life, break into the family prayers, create an independence which is not cooperative, causes distortion, limits the family and frustrates the children already born. . . .

I beg of you, you who could and should be bearing and rearing a family: Wives, come home from the typewriter, the laundry, the nursing, come home from the factory, the café.

No career approaches in importance that of wife, homemaker, mother . . .

Come home, wives, to your husbands. Make home a heaven for them. Come home wives, to your children, born and unborn. Wrap the motherly cloak about you and unembarrassed help in a major role to create the bodies for the immortal souls who anxiously wait.

When you have fully complemented your husband in home life and borne the children, growing up full of faith, integrity, responsibility and goodness, then you have achieved your accomplishments supreme, without peer, and you will be the envy through time and eternity.[59]

How do you feel the Lord looks upon those who would trade flesh-and-blood children for pianos or television or furniture or an automobile, and is this not actually the case when people will buy these luxuries and yet cannot afford to have their children?[60]

President Ezra Taft Benson

Take time to always be at the crossroads when your children are either coming or going. . . . Be there at the crossroads whether your children are six or sixteen.[61]

In a home where there is an able-bodied husband, he is expected to be the breadwinner. . . .

Sometimes the mother works outside of the home at the encouragement, or even insistence, of her husband. It is he who wants the items or conveniences that the extra income can buy. Not only will the family suffer in such instances, brethren, but your own spiritual growth and progression will be hampered. . . .

One apparent impact of the women's movement has been the feelings of discontent it has created among young women who have chosen the role of wife and mother. . . . This view loses sight of the eternal perspective.[62]

There are voices in our midst which would attempt to convince you that these home-centered truths are not applicable to our present-day conditions. If you listen and heed, you will be lured away from your principal obligations.

Beguiling voices in the world cry out for "alternative life-styles" for women. They maintain that some women are better suited for careers than for marriage and motherhood.

These individuals spread their discontent by the propaganda that there are more exciting and self-fulfilling roles for women than home-making. Some even have been bold to suggest that the Church move away from the 'Mormon woman stereotype' of homemaking and rearing children. They also say it is wise to limit your family so you can have more time for personal goals and self-fulfillment.[63]

The first priority for a woman is to prepare herself for her divine and eternal mission, whether she is married soon or late.[64]

It is time that the hearts of us fathers be turned to our children and the hearts of the children be turned to us fathers, or we shall both be cursed. The seeds of divorce are often sown and the blessings of children delayed by wives working outside the home. Working mothers should remember that their children usually need more of mother than of money.[65]

President Howard W. Hunter

You who hold the priesthood have the responsibility, unless disabled, to provide temporal support for your wife and children. No man can shift the burden of responsibility to another, not even to his wife. The Lord has commanded that women and children have claim on their husbands and fathers for their maintenance (see D&C 83 ; 1 Timothy 5:8). President Ezra Taft Benson has stated that when a husband encourages or insists that his wife work out of the home for their convenience, "not only will the family suffer in such instances, . . . but [his] own spiritual growth and progression will be hampered."[66]

President Gordon B. Hinckley

I think the nurture and upbringing of children is more than a part-time responsibility. I recognize that some women must work, but I fear that there are far too many who do so only to get the means for a little more luxury and a few fancier toys.

Families are being torn asunder everywhere. Family relationships are strained as women try to keep up with the rigors of two full-time jobs.[67]

Some years ago President Benson delivered a message to the women of the Church. He encouraged them to leave their employment and give their individual time to their children. I sustain the position which he took.

Nevertheless, I recognize, as he recognized, that there are some women (it has become very many, in fact) who have to work to provide for the needs of their families. To you I say, do the very best you can. I hope that if you are employed full-time you are doing it to ensure that basic needs are met and not simply to indulge a taste for an elaborate home, fancy cars, and other luxuries.

It is well-nigh impossible to be a full-time homemaker and a full-time employee.[68]

To you women who find it necessary to work when you would rather be at home, may I speak briefly. I know that there are many of you who find yourselves in this situation. Some of you have been abandoned and are divorced, with children to care for. Some of you are widows with dependent families. I honor you and respect you for your integrity and spirit of self-reliance. I pray that the Lord will bless you with strength and great capacity, for you need both.[69]

Correlation Department

From 1995 to 2000, I was assigned as a curriculum writer for the seminaries and institutes and asked to write and compile the manual *Eternal Marriage Student Manual,* from which the previous quotes are taken. Our team also wrote the *Religion 234–235 Institute Teacher's Manual* to go with the student manual. We regularly submitted our work to the Church Correlation Department for review.

I recall one of the many helpful comments that came back to me from Correlation concerning the previous quotes and the corresponding lesson on mothers working outside of their homes. The reviewer suggested that whenever teaching these ideas that we emphasize Elder Richard G. Scott's counsel on the topic. Elder Scott first quoted President Benson and then added the idea that one Correlation reviewer felt was incredibly important:

President Benson has taught that a mother with children should be in the home. He also said, "We realize . . . that some of our choice sisters are widowed and divorced and that others find themselves in unusual circumstances where, out of necessity, they are required to work for a period of time. But these instances are the exception, not the rule" (Ezra Taft Benson, *To the Mothers in Zion* [pamphlet, 1987], 5–6). *You in these unusual circumstances qualify for additional inspiration and strength from the Lord. Those who leave the home for lesser reasons will not.*[70] (Emphasis added.)

Over the years, whenever I've taught this lesson, I try to follow Correlation's counsel. I review the quotations from our prophets that emphasize it's a difficult task to try to be a full-time mother and have an outside employment at the same time. However, the Brethren also teach there are a great many women today, through no fault of their own, who find themselves in this situation. It's a situation where some faithful Latter-day Saint mothers might unduly feel guilt and pressure. Elder Scott's counsel set the standard and explained the consequences of our choices in this matter: If you qualify for being in one of these unusual circumstances, then with faith you can ask for and expect "additional inspiration and strength from the Lord." With these great blessings, anything is possible. However, if you choose to leave the home "for lesser reasons," you will not qualify for the needed miracle-making assistance, so you're basically on your own in your pursuits.

Research Findings on Mothers Working Outside the Home

The counsel above given by the Brethren over the years is often criticized and considered out-of-date and even stifling by many outside of the LDS faith, and even by some inside the faith. However, if one honestly and openly looks at the research and facts associated with the issue, you will see that there are proven, serious consequences to marriages, families, and society for turning their backs on this counsel. The data supports the Church's teachings about mothers working outside the home in a variety of ways.

What follows is a summary of research findings about dual-career or dual-earner families. It reviews North American statistics, reasons women work, their economic contribution, the broad effects, costs of working outside the home, and a working mother's effects on children. Frank D. Cox compiled the findings and published them in a textbook I used for introduction to the family classes at BYU.[71] As you review these statistics and findings, keep in mind the consistent counsel of Church leaders over the years:

North American statistics:

1. Around 74 percent of all married mothers with children under age eighteen worked in 1996; 38 percent worked full-time. More than half the mothers with children under age six were either working or looking for work.

2. The U.S. Department of Labor predicts that one half of labor force entrants between 1992 and 2005 will be women. This has created what the Census Bureau now describes as a "husband primary-earner, wife secondary-earner" family.

Reasons cited for the increase of women in the work force:

3. Inflationary pressures and the expectations of a rising standard of living are the two main reasons American women go into the work force. Most married women choose to enter the work force to increase their standard of living rather than out of necessity.

4. Increasing education has contributed to women working outside the home.

5. Attitudes about the role of women in the family have changed greatly during this century. Many women today believe that working outside the home is important for personal satisfaction rather than just for earning additional money.

The working wife's economic contribution to the family:

6. In general, working mothers spend between 25 to 50 percent of their income on work-related expenses, depending upon the type of work and age of their children and other factors.

7. Dual-earner families with a median income and two children average 35 percent for the wife's net contribution to family income. Wives working part-time increase the family income on the average of 29 percent for median income families. Full-time working wives increase family income by about 70 percent in low income families.

Broad effects:

8. Gender roles are less clear and more overlapping in dual-earner families. Role conflict and ambiguity are exaggerated when both partners work.

9. Power within the family is redistributed as both partners contribute monetarily to the families support.

10. Family activities and timetables are more restrictive.

11. Many mothers try to become "supermoms" as they cope with both family responsibilities and an outside career.

12. Birthrates have declined.

The costs of mothers working outside the home:

13. There are women with children who are beginning to return to full-time motherhood if they are able to afford it. "The ideal of the 1980s supermom who does it all at home and at work no longer seems realistic for these women. As one person puts it, 'Supermom has come down with chronic fatigue syndrome.' These women also feel that their children need more attention."

14. Some of the decrease in the earnings gap between men and women is because of reduced wages for men. This trend is partially responsible for the economic need of some wives to work. The family must have the second paycheck in order just to survive.

15. Mothers with children at home average about thirty-six hours a week working in the home. Meal preparation and cleanup is about 30 percent, care of family members 15–25 percent, and clothing and regular house care is about 15 percent. When they go to work outside the home, the amount of work to be done at home remains the same. It must be done and mothers still do it.

16. Most husbands do not make up the difference in housework when wives work. Husbands are fairly likely to agree that they should do more in their households, but they rarely live up to what they say they will do, or to their wives' expectations.

Husbands doing housework spend between four and six hours per week, or about 14 percent of the total amount that needs to be done.

17. Time spent with family is a precious commodity for working mothers. The most common complaint of working mothers is their lack of time for recreation, vacation trips, picnics, children, intimacy, and leisure time.

18. The work overload leads women to feel resentful and put upon if their husband and family do not meet their expectations for help. This may be one of the major factors in America's increased divorce rate.

19. Employment overload is typical for the self-employed and those in management positions. Approximately 30 percent of both men and women now work on weekends. The average American worker puts in forty-six hours a week at the office and six more hours at home for a total of fifty-two hours.

20. A working woman is more likely to postpone marriage because she is able to support herself. Marriage rates have dropped since 1955, and age at first marriage has also risen for both women and men.

21. Most careers require relocation for promotion. Dual-career families experience stress when one of the working spouses is asked to move.

22. Dual-career families have twice the job insecurity and vulnerability to family economic upheaval that is caused from forced unemployment.

23. If both partners are successful in their careers, it usually means that major career decisions will have to be made periodically throughout the relationship. Each new decision may upset the balance that the couple has previously worked out.

The effects on children:

24. According to one estimate, the amounts of total contact parents have with their children has dropped 40 percent since 1965.

25. American parents believe that spending less time with their families is the most important cause of fragmentation and stress in contemporary family life.

26. Researchers who observed four hundred childcare centers in several different states concluded that only one in seven centers were of good quality, where children enjoyed close relationships with adults and teachers who focused on the individual needs of the children.

27. These same researchers found that parents greatly overestimated the care that was being given to their children.

28. Consistency and predictability are two crucial attributes to the development of young children. Many parents use a number of childcare providers rather than just one, making consistency and predictability in their children's lives difficult.

29. The type of role behavior expected on the job and in the family may be incompatible. A manager at work is often expected to be self-reliant, emotionally stable, aggressive, and objective. Family members often need a wife and mother who is warm, nurturing, emotional, and vulnerable in their interactions.

30. Dual-career families have fewer children than traditional families.

Conclusion:

These statistics about and findings of what happens when mothers work outside the home should not be surprising to any Latter-day Saint who has followed the teachings of the prophets on this topic since 1972. The questions that should be asked by each of us are, "Is it necessary? Does our situation qualify us for help from on high? If not, how much of a price are we willing to pay to be able to acquire the world's indices of material success? Will it be worth it in the long run, particularly with children?"

President Gordon B. Hinckley said, "In terms of your happiness, in terms of the matters that make you proud or sad, nothing—I repeat, nothing—will have so profound an effect on you as the way your children turn out."[72]

Women and Education

The fact that Church leaders have encouraged mothers with children at home to remain in the home does not mean they devalue education for women. Elder Howard W. Hunter taught, "There are impelling reasons for our sisters to plan toward employment also. We want them to obtain all the education and vocational training possible before marriage. If they become widowed or divorced and need to work, we want them to have dignified and rewarding employment. If a sister does not marry, she has every right to engage in a profession that allows her to magnify her talents and gifts."[73]

I listed nearly fifty different skills my wife used to rear our eight children. Though she never had to professionally use the modern dance education she received at the University of Utah, she learned how to master those skills. There is far more value to higher education for women than gaining marketable economic skills and using education skills as an insurance policy in case they become single again.

It's been said that the maternal influence is the leading factor over whether children choose to stay in school and then go on to higher education or not. Mothers have the potential to play the most important role of educator in a child's early life, and as they get older they are still the heart of the child's attitude about education.

Critics of stay-at-home mothers often site they've "wasted" their talents and could have made more significant contributions. I counter that argument again with the example of my wife and children, and others like her who made the same choices. They devoted their lives to making their children ready for the world spiritually, intellectually, physically, and socially and thus made the world a better place. I don't think my wife wasted her college education by being there for our children when they needed her.

As a result of this immense dedication and work, all our children have college degrees and skills to contribute to society. All pay taxes and none are in jail or consuming other people's tax dollars for their support. Together, they are doing far more than any one woman could have ever dreamed of doing on her own. My wife and mothers like her multiply their power for good by each child they bring into the world and responsibly nurture to maturity. The value of the work a mother does within the walls of her own home should never be underestimated or scoffed at by anyone.

Summary

Since the Fall in the Garden of Eden, mankind has been required to work to survive. A marriage is also like a garden—a post-Eden garden complete with reoccurring briars, weeds, and thorns. Any intimate relationship has to be attended to on a regular basis if a happy and productive harvest is expected. Hard work is required at every stage of the relationship to consistently keep your true love for all of eternity.

For singles to find the perfect eternal mate, they need to work hard to become the perfect mate that someone would want to date. Men need to resist the modern tendency of accepting less and less responsibility in dating and marriage and take the initiative in the dating game and work to prepare themselves for obtaining gainful employment. The provider role for men is an important part of the plan of salvation and should not be abdicated to their wives under normal circumstances.

All prophets since Spencer W. Kimball have consistently taught the importance of mothers being allowed to stay in the home when possible. Research data verifies the wisdom and benefits of this position. The Church continues to stress the importance of education for both men and women.

The Principle of Work Self-Evaluation Questions for Men

- If you are single, are you actively working toward finding an eternal mate?

- Are you willing to do the hard work necessary to successfully honor the roles of husband, father, patriarch, and priesthood holder?
- Are you willing to do the work necessary to preside, protect, and provide for your eternal family?
- Are you willing to work long and hard enough to allow your wife (or future wife) to stay home with the children if she so chooses?

The Principle of Work Self-Evaluation Questions for Women

- If you are single, are you working to prepare yourself for an eternal marriage and family when the opportunity presents itself?
- If married, is the work you're engaged in the most meaningful and rewarding thing you could be doing?

Chapter 11: Wholesome Recreational Activities

Successful marriages and families are established and maintained on the principle of wholesome recreational activities.

Understanding the Principle of Wholesome Recreation

Charles Francis Adams (August 18, 1808–November 21, 1886) was a grandson of John Adams, second president of the United States, and the son of John Quincy Adams, the sixth president. He was a lawyer, diplomat (ambassador to Great Britain), and writer. In other words, he was a busy man with little free time. Despite his busy life, he took his son fishing one day. In his diary, he wrote, "Went fishing with my son today. A day wasted." On that same day, his son wrote in his diary, "Went fishing with my father today, the most wonderful day of my life."[74]

The Need for Balance

Many activities will be considered by some to be work and others to be recreation. To me, gardening is work: hard and essential. To my wife, it's an escape that's fun, and she can't wait to get out of the house to her garden sanctuary. To a professional photographer, going to work each day may get old. I as an amateur photographer anxiously anticipate each opportunity to take a break, go somewhere, and photograph something new.

Nearly any wholesome activity could be considered recreation if it implies participation to be healthy and refreshing to mind and body. I'm sure the Brethren included the word *wholesome* in the proclamation for a reason. If not, I could see some Latter-day Saints using the proclamation to justify taking a wad of cash and heading for the consumption parts of Las Vegas. The large and spacious building in Lehi's dream is basically a recreational facility—one of non-wholesome leisure activities that do not healthily refresh either the mind or the body. Hence why the term *wholesome* in this principle is important.

The leaders of the Church have long recognized the need for a healthy balance in our lives. Even on the long and arduous journeys west by the pioneers, dancing and singing were performed many nights by the light of the campfires. When the foundations for Salt Lake City were first laid out, some of the first public buildings constructed were theaters where plays were performed and cultural halls where dances could be held. The practice continues today in ward and stake houses throughout the world as nearly all have cultural halls for athletic competitions and other events.

From the writings of Church leaders, we can find both counsel to participate in wholesome recreation and warnings to keep all things in proper balance:

President Spencer W. Kimball

"Too much leisure for children leaves them in a state of boredom, and it is natural for them to want more and more of the expensive things for their recreation. We must bring dignity to labor in sharing the responsibilities of the home and the yard" (*Ensign*, May 1976, 5).

President Ezra Taft Benson

"Wholesome recreation is part of our religion, and a change of pace is necessary, and even its anticipation can lift the spirit" (*Ensign*, November 1974, 6).

"Successful families do things together: family projects, work, vacations, recreation, and reunions" (*Ensign*, May 1984, 6).

Elder James E. Faust

"*Develop family traditions.* Some of the great strengths of families can be found in their own traditions, which may consist of many things: making special occasions of the blessing of children, baptisms, ordinations to the priesthood, birthdays, fishing trips, skits on Christmas Eve, family home evening, and so forth. The traditions of each family are unique and are provided in large measure by the mother's imprint" (*Ensign*, May 1983, 41).

Elder Joe J. Christensen

"Keep your courtship alive. Make time to do things together—just the two of you. As important as it is to be with the children as a family, you need regular weekly time alone together. Scheduling it will let your children know that you feel that your marriage is so important that you need to nurture it. That takes commitment, planning, and scheduling" (*Ensign*, May 1995, 65).

Just as keeping a proper balance between production and consumption is important for children, it is also important when they grow up. I worked for a home building company that built over four hundred homes a year. I did this for two years. The president of the company was a friend, and I had the opportunity to observe him daily on the job and often with his family.

His work was stressful and competitive and he put in many long, hard hours to make his company profitable. He developed the routine of regularly taking at least a week off every three months to get away and refresh his mind and body. My family and I would occasionally accompany him and his family on these retreats.

The transformation that took place in his personality from these adventures was amazing. At about six weeks since his last vacation and six weeks to go before his next break, he became close to unbearable at work. Because he was the boss and everyone needed his or her job, he could get away with his grumpiness and the employees just tried to stay clear of him until the next vacation.

About ten days before the next recreational activity date, he started to transform day by day into a happy, reasonable person again. When he returned from the activity, he was delightful to be with for the next four to six weeks, and then the cycle started over again.

I was privileged to serve in the Southern Australian Mission under Elder Bruce R. McConkie. Times and mission rules have changed since the 1960s, but some of the fondest memories of my mission were the occasional recreations President McConkie allowed and organized as rewards for reaching mission goals. President McConkie believed in hard work and allowing us to refresh mind and body in wholesome recreational activities.

Wholesome Recreational Activities in Dating and Courtship

The family proclamation states, "Successful marriages and families are established and maintained on principles of . . . wholesome recreational activities." Wholesome recreation for dating couples appears to be divinely approved and recommended. As America has never had arranged marriages or even a chaperone system, modern youth are expected to figure out how to *establish* a relationship on their own through dating activities.

Dating in America for the most part is now done in recreational activities. Following WWI, two things made modern dating patterns possible: the emancipation of women and the mobility made possible by the car. It also became easier for boys to meet girls as the population moved from the farms to the cities and both began going to the same elementary and secondary schools together rather than being separated for most of their formative years.

The types of things people consider recreation and the behavior they exhibit during these activities can tell you a lot about your compatibility with potential mates. Two young ladies in an institute class told of a blind double date they went on one weekend. They were picked up by their dates and told for the first time that their date activity was to go to the batting cages. The girls were wearing dresses. This was strike one for the boys.

When they got there, the young men sat them down to watch while they batted balls from a pitching machine in a fenced-in area. They carried on with the activity for over an hour, just enjoying themselves and getting sweaty. This was strike two.

Finally, the boys became thirsty because of the activity and excused themselves to get drinks. The girls thought at least they would get drinks out of this fiasco of a date, but the boys came back with refreshments only for themselves. Strike three.

The girls called a friend to come get them and left. The boys didn't even notice them leaving. The young women learned a lot about these young men that night—mainly to never speak to them again and to be more careful about accepting blind dates in the future.

In determining couple compatibility, it's important to experience a variety of activities. A dislike of classical music and a refusal to attend concerts and cultural events could be a deal breaker for someone. And someone else could be highly involved in sports, both participating in and watching them, and wants a companion with similar interests to share the experience with.

In addition, dating should include activities not normally seen as recreation. What can you learn about someone by your attending Church together? Invite him to help babysit and see if he panics around children. Will she go with you on a service project? Will any of these findings lead to a deal breaker of some sort? Maybe, maybe not. Sometimes it takes a lot of different kinds of dates with different people to find someone who is compatible in interests and values with you. And some might just get lucky as I did and find them the first day of college.

How important is it to have a variety of different types of activities you can enjoy doing with a potential mate? The similarity principle discussed in chapter one states, "The more alike two people are in intimate relationships (such as dating, courtship, and marriage), the greater the probability that the relationship will succeed." According to this principle, those things matter. How much do these recreational pursuits matter to the overall success of a marriage? That may depend on the personality of the couple and the stage of the marriage.

Wholesome Recreational Activities in Marriage

In youthful years, recreation may be more important to a couple than later in life. It's a fact of life that both our bodies and our interests change over time. Children and additional responsibilities can slow down an athletic woman and her time for sports and leisure time. A career, children, stress, age, and too much pizza can slow down an athletic man. An accident, illness, or financial pressures can slow anyone down.

Even if we stay healthy, sometimes we can no longer afford what we used to do. I can remember when a student all-day lift pass to snow ski was six dollars and we didn't have eight children. When the kids came and ski pass prices inflated, we asked "Now what?" We did more sledding in the winter and hiked the mountains in the summer. The kids were missing expensive European vacations and ski trips but still turned out just fine without them.

If the marriage is based primarily around specific activities that can no longer be participated in, can the marriage last? The answer is yes if you're creative and don't insist on keeping up with the Jones, and if the other nine principles this book is based on are solid parts of the marriage relationship.

My wife and I loved to water and snow ski together in our early years. It was an important part of our dating and courtship years. We have continued to ski together ever since. We took a picture on our fortieth wedding anniversary of us waterskiing together with the Idaho Falls Temple in the background, where we were married. What the picture doesn't show is how many times it took us to pull up at the same time with each of us on one ski. At the time of this writing, we are still both water and snow skiing together and are enjoying it more at slower speeds and less often.

We still enjoy traveling across America with a travel trailer as well as hiking in the mountains, going to movies occasionally, eating out, and traveling to visit grandchildren's ball games, recitals, graduations, baptisms, blessings, and so on. I'm a lot like my old boss—after about six weeks, I feel the need for a break.

It's fun to observe long-retired couples with season tickets going to college football and basketball games together. The best seats in the stadium seem to be occupied mostly by senior couples. A news article in the fall of 2011 featured a couple that enjoyed season football and basketball tickets at the University of Utah every year since 1945. For fifty-seven straight years, the couple enjoyed the ball games together until the husband died in 2003. The wife, age eighty-eight, in 2011 still attended the games with a son.

I contrast the enjoyment this couple had for all those years with another couple I heard about who are close to the same age. The wife loved to watch football and basketball and would like to have had season tickets to BYU for the past fifty years. The husband, however, hated to watch sports, so they never attended any football or basketball games together.

The husband, however, loved to travel, but his wife did not, so they stayed close to home for their vacations for those same fifty years. They stayed married and are on their way to the celestial kingdom because, as a couple, they perfected the principles of faith, prayer, repentance, forgiveness, respect, love, compassion, and work. However, both missed out on a lot of chances to renew body and spirit together in the wholesome recreational activities that each enjoyed. If they had been willing to compromise and sacrifice a little, both could have been happier.

I recall a story about a well-known chemistry professor I had in college dutifully attending a Utah symphony concert with his wife because she enjoyed them and he wanted to please her. During the concert, he smiled and listened to the music while discreetly working out chemistry problems on the back of the program.

A well-rounded marriage is like a ten-spoke wheel on a bicycle. If one or more of the spokes is too short, the wheel will have a flat spot on it. Compatible wholesome recreational activities are one of the ten spokes on the wheel. It will still work and can get you where you want to go; it's just not as smooth a ride nor as much fun as it could be if the wheel were perfectly round.

Summary

The term *wholesome recreation* implies participation in activities that are healthy and refreshing mind and body. Dating couples engage in wholesome recreational activities to learn about the compatibility of a potential mate and to "establish" a marriage.

Church leaders have consistently encouraged married couples to continue to court and renew ("maintain") affectionate feelings throughout the marriage. Families need to consistently budget time and money to build traditions of wholesome recreational activities together. Ideally, these activities are those that both partners can enjoy, but sometimes unselfish compromise, and a little sacrifice for the happiness of one's eternal mate may be necessary.

Church leaders have also counseled members not to be excessive in recreational pursuits and to budget wisely for them without going into debt. Moderation and a proper balance in recreation and work activities make for a more satisfying and productive life.

Wholesome Recreational Activities
Self-Evaluation Questions

- Do you feel you have a proper balance in your life between those things you have to do and wholesome recreational pursuits?
  A. Yes
  B. No

- Do your recreational breaks lead to a "healthy refreshing mind and body"?
  A. Yes
  B. No

- Are your recreational activities and equipment within reasonable budget goals?
  A. Yes
  B. Close
  C. It's a little out of control

- Are you willing to occasionally do recreational activities that are of more interest to your partner than they are to you?
  A. Yes
  B. No

- Make a list of things you do on a regular basis for recreation. How many of these include your spouse?
  A. Most of them
  B. Enough that there's no resentment
  C. Few or none

This completes our discussion of the ten foundational principles for establishing and maintaining a marriage and family that can last through all eternity. The ten principles were identified and organized as such by modern prophets, seers, and revelators in 1995, who testified to their truth, effectiveness, and importance. I greatly appreciate their wisdom and efforts made to share these precious pearls of great price with us and the world.

I wish you well in your pursuit of happiness and the fulness of joy that can only be found in eternal marriages and families. I have included two appendices that follow for readers who wish to review the doctrines dealing with eternal relationships as found in the plan of salvation, or the great plan of happiness, re-revealed to Joseph Smith in the last dispensation.

Sometimes it helps to review why we are working so hard to keep marriages and families together. Without an eternal perspective of our daily lives, problems and weaknesses can lead to us making serious mistakes. I testify that there is a potential eternity of happiness just on the other side of the thin veil that temporarily separates us from our heavenly parents. They want us to return to Them with honor and become heirs in Their kingdom. Helping us return to Them is Their work and Their glory. An eternity of joy is our divine destiny and is waiting for us if we can not only endure to the end, but also learn to enjoy the trip all the way there.

Appendix 1: The Foundation Doctrine for Eternal Love

William Wordsworth wrote these immortal words: "Trailing clouds of glory do we come / From God, who is our home: / Heaven lies about us in our infancy!"[75] What is the purpose of our existence?

We live in a world today where comparatively few people understand basic questions mankind should know: Who are we? Where did we come from? What is the purpose of our existence? True love and the resulting strong marriages and families based on this knowledge are becoming casualties of this ever-increasing ignorance of our heritage and potential. It's rather ironic that this basic knowledge of our birthright as children of God and the purpose of our lives would be in such decline in the midst of the "information age" and powerful knowledge-gathering technologies.

The Deteriorating Family and the Proclamation

"The Family: A Proclamation to the World" teaches that the family is central to our understanding of who we are, where we came from, and what the purpose of our existence is. Yet in these postmodern times, there's evidence that the traditional family is moving toward extinction at a fairly rapid rate.

I show my BYU students a documentary that was produced in 2008 entitled *Demographic Winter: the Decline of the Human Family*.[76] In it, well-respected scholars from the fields of demography (the statistical study of human populations), economics, and the social sciences are interviewed. The demographers show statistics that chart an ever-declining fertility rate worldwide, which they term *demographic winter*. The social scientists theorize the causes of the decline and the social consequences of it. The economists show the catastrophic monetary effects these changes will produce. A summary of some of these modern trends includes:

- Fewer and fewer people each year see the need to marry.
- Those who do marry are having fewer children, leading to a birth dearth in Europe, Canada, South America, and—to a slightly lesser degree—the United States.
- Around sixty percent of the population growth of the United States since 1990 has come from immigrants and their children, mostly Hispanic.
- When fewer children are born, there are proportionately more elderly, resulting in what is called an aging population.
- Economic projections based upon an aging and then declining population predict grave consequences. Never in history have we had economic prosperity following depopulation.
- Social Security, Medicare, and Medicaid all face an increasingly uncertain future as younger workers are being asked to support more and more of the retired population.
- There is a demographic economic paradox created as those who can best sustain a large family are not having those large families and those who can least sustain large families have more children. The results are that fewer children born today will be responsibly prepared to make positive economic contributions in the future. At least 25 percent of the children born today will not be prepared to earn a living.
- There's the real possibility that future generations will experience less prosperity than their parents had.

The documentary's authors give five reasons for the birth dearth and its dire, imminent consequences:

- *Cohabitation.* There is a rising rate of cohabitation. Cohabitating couples tend to have fewer children than married couples and, if they do marry, they do so much later in life. One of the biggest reasons for the low fertility rate is people having children too late in their lives.

- *Divorce.* The divorce revolution has meant that neither men nor women can count on their spouses being there for them in the future. The risk of divorce a couple faces decreases the chances that they'll have another child.

- *Sexual revolution.* The sexual revolution separated sex from the responsibility of marriage and children. For multiple reasons, social scientists believe that the sexual revolution had both direct and indirect effects on fertility decline.

- *Working mothers.* The more successful that women become in the workplace before they have their children, the higher the opportunity costs them when they have children. They find it harder to leave work and have children.

- *Prosperity.* Economists tell us that as countries and individuals become prosperous, they tend to desire fewer children.

There you have it: disrespecting marriage, easy divorce, sexual irresponsibility, mothers working outside the home, and prosperity cause misplaced priorities. All these causes are themselves caused by the lack of an eternal perspective of where we came from, who we are, and what our potential is.

The end result is there are fewer and fewer couples in the world each year discovering and enjoying the fruits of true love that lead to marriage and family.

The First Presidency and the Quorum of Twelve Apostles of The Church of Jesus Christ of Latter-day Saints issued this solemn warning in 1995: "Further we warn that the disintegration of the family will bring upon individuals, communities, and nations the calamities foretold by ancient and modern prophets."[77] The consequences listed above will all lead to the disintegration of the family. The behavioral causes of the consequences listed above are all warned against in this proclamation to the world.

Without knowledge of the great plan of happiness as our foundation for true love, it is easy to fall victim to any or all of these last days' deceptions. The plan of salvation answers the three questions man has asked from the beginning of time.

Here are the short answers to the three questions:

Who are we? We are the offspring of deity born as spirit children.

Where did we come from? We came from a premortal existence where we lived with our heavenly parents and learned directly from Them. In that existence, we had a choice between Heavenly Father and Jesus Christ's plan for our progression and Lucifer's plan to take away our agency and force obedience. All of us here on earth chose Father's plan.

Why are we here? Earth was created as a final exam of sorts, a testing ground for those who chose Heavenly Father's plan. We have been sent here to learn about ourselves and see if we want the responsibilities and glory of godhood. It's an amazing claim. Satan has done all he can over the ages to keep our true potential hidden from us. To not understand this potential is to make us vulnerable to the deceptions and consequences described previously.

Let's review the basics of God's plan for man and our true potential, as well as what it takes to reach this potential. It's when we understand this idea that we see clearly the reward for taking the time and effort to learn to consistently lay the foundations for true, eternal love.

Exaltation

Our potential is stated most simply with President Lorenzo Snow's oft-repeated statement: "As man now is, God once was; as God now is, man may be." President Heber J. Grant and his counselors, Anthony W. Ivins and Charles W. Nibley, issued a more detailed description of this LDS doctrine. "Man is the child of God, formed in the divine image and endowed with divine attributes, and even as the infant son of an earthly father and mother is capable in due time of becoming a man, so that undeveloped offspring of celestial parentage is capable, by experience through ages and aeons, of evolving into a God."[78]

Divine Nature and Destiny

The family proclamation adds more detail: "All human beings—male and female—are created in the image of God. Each is a beloved spirit son or daughter of heavenly parents, and, as such, each has a *divine nature* and *destiny*" (emphasis added). To me, "divine nature" means we are created in the image and likeness of our heavenly parents and have something like their DNA in our bones. Part of our divine nature is our inheritance by simply being children of God, capable of becoming like our parents. "Divine destiny" seems to refer to our potential for greatness. Church leaders often use the terms interchangeably when they are addressing the topic.

President Gordon B. Hinckley said,

> There is something of divinity within each of you. You have such tremendous potential with that quality as a part of your inherited nature. Every one of you was endowed by your Father in Heaven with a tremendous capacity to do good in the world.
>
> Train your minds and your hands that you may be equipped to serve well in the society of which you are a part. Cultivate the art of being kind, of being thoughtful, of being helpful. Refine within you the quality of mercy which comes as a part of the divine attributes you have inherited.[79]

In Greek, "divine destiny" is an adjective: *theios*. One of the possible definitions is whatever can in any respect be likened to God, or resembles Him in any way. Easton defines *divine destiny* as "godliness." It is the whole of practical piety (1 Timothy 4:8; 2 Peter 1:6). "It supposes knowledge, veneration, affection, dependence, submission, gratitude, and obedience." In 1 Timothy 3:16, it denotes the substance of revealed religion.[80]

One could say our divine destiny basically consists of three things: glory, immortality, and eternal lives. Brigham Young taught, "The gospel and the priesthood are the means he employs to save and exalt his obedient children to the possession with him of the same glory and power to be crowned with crowns of glory, immortality and eternal lives."[81] *Glory* means to become an heir to the glory of God, a term that denotes the fulness of the majesty of God. *Immortality* is unending life and enduring fame, whereas *eternal lives* refer to an eternal increase of our own spirit children. I believe this is our divine nature and our divine destiny.

Discipline, Divine Destiny, and Pure Love

Our divine nature and destiny gives us the potential and ability to progress, evolve, and become like our first parents if we will but follow the path God has set out for us. Joseph Smith, by divine revelation, taught, "God himself, finding he was in the midst of spirits and glory, because he was more intelligent, saw proper to institute laws whereby the rest could have a privilege to advance like himself" ("The King Follett Sermon, *Ensign*, May 1971). Our Heavenly Father's work and glory is to help and encourage, but He will not force us to achieve the same glory, immortality, and eternal life He has. This is our divine destiny; this is man's potential. It has to be worked toward. Learning perfect and pure love, as God possesses, is crucial to this process.

In 2 Peter 1:4, we read, "Whereby are given unto us exceeding great and precious promises; that by these ye might be partakers of the divine nature, having escaped the corruption that is in the world through lust." Part of the process of becoming one with God is the discipline it takes to escape the corruption of this world that comes from our natural man lusts and desires. Many of these lusts are the ones described by Paul in 2 Timothy 3:1–6.

Just as it takes discipline and practice to better your score in golf, bowling, or archery, discipline is also an important part of the price of achieving pure love and achieving divine nature. In order to benefit from the principles presented in these chapters, readers will need to be willing to discipline themselves in areas where they discover improvement is needed. There may be a little pain before the gain is realized. Such is often the way of life.

The pain comes from having to discard old habits that have almost become our friends and enablers over the years. We are familiar with them and comfortable around them, even though we know deep down that they can destroy us. It may take insight, courage, and studied and measured discipline to separate ourselves from these self-destructive patterns.

Sin in a variety of forms is one type of those habits that destroy relationships. Orson Pratt taught the importance of disciplining the lusts of the flesh and its opposition to pure love: "The more righteous a people become the more they are qualified for loving others and rendering them happy. A wicked man can have but little love for his wife."[82]

Finding and keeping pure, eternal love requires moral discipline. The tempting modern-day corruption feeds lust and destroys our ability to use our inherited divine nature talents to reach our divine destiny as heirs of God. President James E. Faust taught, "As the scales of worldliness are taken from our eyes, we see more clearly who we are and what our responsibilities are concerning our divine destiny."[83]

Alma taught the same idea: "And also see that ye bridle all your passions, that ye may be filled with love" (Alma 38:12). The reverse could also be inferred from this passage. When we are filled with perfect love, we can bridle all our passions.

Apotheosis of Man

Some today are critical of Latter-day Saints for believing in our divine nature and destiny and the possibility of becoming like unto our heavenly parents. If examined closely, however, it may not be such a radical idea. There is good evidence that many faith groups around the world once believed in the apotheosis of man. *Apotheosis* (from the Greek word *apotheoun*, which means "to deify") refers to the exaltation of a subject to divine level. In theology, the term *apotheosis* means that an individual can be raised to godlike stature and glory.

This idea is depicted in a large fresco that was painted in 1856, visible through the oculus of the dome in the rotunda of the United States Capitol Building. It visualizes the apotheosis of George Washington. Washington is dressed in a purple robe, denoting royalty, as he becomes a god. (See image on the next page.)

A similar doctrine is expressed in the patristic writings or the Christian writings of church "fathers" in the first few centuries after Christ's death and Resurrection and the death of the Apostles. The doctrine is referred to as divinization. Author Jonathan Jacobs gave examples of some of these writings:

- St. Irenaeus of Lyons stated that God "became what we are in order to make us what he is himself."

- St. Athanasius wrote that "God became man so that men might become gods."
- St. Cyril of Alexandria said that we "are called 'temples of God' and indeed 'gods,' and so we are."
- St. Basil the Great stated that "becoming a god" is the highest goal of all.
- St. Gregory of Nazianzus implored us to "become gods for (God's) sake, since (God) became man for our sake."[84]

The apotheosis or divinization of man is an idea that is older than the earth. We start to become one with God when we acknowledge His existence and our dependence upon Him, commit ourselves to learning and keeping His commandments, and strive to emulate His character and values. Reaching the target of true love in this life and the next cannot be reached unless we understand this glorious doctrine and strive to achieve it.

Apotheosis of President George Washington,
rotunda of the U.S. Capitol Building.

Biblical Evidence for Our Divine Nature and Destiny

The following are a couple biblical references by Apostles Paul and John the Beloved that show the early Church founded by Christ taught that we are children of God with a divine nature and destiny and, if we manage to overcome all things, can become joint-heirs with Christ:

In 1 John 3:2, John testified we are "sons of God," whose potential is not reached in mortality. However, when the Savior comes again, those who have had the faith to purify themselves can become like Him. "Beloved, now are we the sons of God, and it doth not yet appear what we shall be: but we know that, when he shall appear, we shall be like him; for we shall see him as he is. And every man that hath this hope in him purifieth himself, even as he is pure."

Paul taught in Romans 8:14, 16–17 that the Spirit can lead us to understand our inheritance as sons of God and, as such, we have the potential to be "joint-heirs with Christ." An heir is someone who receives an inheritance. What else could these scripture verses be saying? "For as many as are led by the Spirit of God, they are the sons of God. . . . The Spirit itself beareth witness with our spirit, that we are the children of God: And if children, then heirs; heirs of God, and joint-heirs with Christ; if so be that we suffer with [Him], that we may be also glorified together."

In Galatians 3:26, 29, Paul again taught the idea that humans are children of God and heirs of promise. "For ye are all the children of God by faith in Christ Jesus. And if ye [be] Christ's, then are ye Abraham's seed, and heirs according to the promise."

In Galatians 4:7, Paul discussed the progression we go through as we follow the path that God sets out for us to become like Him. We start as servants, helping God in His work, and progress to the status of a son with inheritance rights. "Wherefore thou art no more a servant, but a son; and if a son, then an heir of God through Christ."

In Revelation 1:6, John praised God for making it possible for us to become like Him: "And hath made us kings and priests unto God, and his Father; to him be glory and dominion for ever and ever. Amen."

In Revelation 3:21 and 21:7, John explained the discipline necessary for us to become like God. Revelation 3:21 reads, "To him that overcometh will I grant to sit with me in my throne, even as I also overcame, and am set down with my Father in his throne." Revelation 21:7 says, "He that overcometh shall inherit all things; and I will be his God, and he shall be my son."

Opposition to the Plan

Joseph Smith, as recorded by Wilford Woodruff, taught a similar concept in his definition of salvation: "Salvation is nothing more nor less than the triumph over all our enemies in this world and over all evil spirits in the world to come."[85]

There are forces at work today that will, if left unchecked, cause the disintegration of true love, marriage, and the family, bringing upon us the "calamities foretold by ancient and modern prophets." The power behind the forces causing this disintegration can be explained by just one scripture: "And the love of men shall wax cold, and iniquity shall abound" (D&C 45:27).

Iniquity destroys true love. Iniquity abounds because mankind lacks the eternal perspective to choose God's plan over Satan's seductive distractions. These patterns have been going on since man was placed on the earth: "And Satan came among them, saying: I am also a son of God; and he commanded them, saying: Believe it not; and they believed it not, and they loved Satan more than God. And men began from that time forth to be carnal, sensual, and devilish" (Moses 5:13).

The end result of unchecked iniquity is always the destruction of any civilization that evolves to that point. Noah's dispensation, Sodom and Gomorra, ancient Israel, Rome and Greece, the Nephites and Lamanites, and more recently Nazi Germany. There was a worldwide destruction of the wicked in the days of Noah by flood and there will be another—this time by fire—in our times, the last days.

Summary

There is a plan to save those willing to listen from the perils of the last days and the coming destruction of the wicked. Happiness in marriage and family life is possible and even probable if we follow the path and plan that leads to it.

The earth must be flooded with knowledge of God's great plan of happiness and the believers must gather to the stakes of Zion for safety. The children of Zion need to learn or relearn who they are, where they came from, and what their divine nature and destinies are. This appendix addressed those questions. The next one examines the price that must be paid to reach this promised safety, achieve our full potential as children of God, and find true love.

Appendix 2: The Three Great Unities of Eternal Love

To achieve true love, reach our full divine potential, and take advantage of what God is offering us in his great plan of happiness requires us to achieve three great unities. Each unity involves study, prayer, discovery, commitment, and specific actions that eventually lead to becoming one. It's not an easy path to choose, but the rewards are incalculable and worth the effort. It's a task that may seem impossible to accomplish. However, if we do all that we can, then our Lord and Savior will do the rest to make it possible, "for we know that it is by grace that we are saved, after all we can do" (2 Nephi 25:23).

Three Great Unities

Again, we must keep in mind that there's a great deceiver working against God's plan for man and our achieving these unities. Satan has successfully hidden his actions and intentions from the world, and few understand his goals and great determination to distract us and seal us as his. President James E. Faust warned Church members in 2007 about this: "I think we will witness increasing evidence of Satan's power as the kingdom of God grows stronger. I believe Satan's ever-expanding efforts are some proof of the truthfulness of this work. In the future the opposition will be both more subtle and more open. It will be masked in greater sophistication and cunning, but it will also be more blatant. We will need greater spirituality to perceive all of the forms of evil and greater strength to resist it."[86]

One of Satan's most important goals is the destruction of traditional marriage and family life. He does this by enticing us to forget who we are, where we came from, and why we are here. Then it is easy to get us to let go of the iron rod or drop the precious fruit and wander on forbidden paths. Latter-day Saints of all races and cultures are not exempt and will be tested by Satan and should know better than this. "For in those days there shall also arise false Christs, and false prophets, and shall show great signs and wonders, insomuch, that, if possible, they shall deceive the very elect, who are the elect according to the covenant" (Joseph Smith—Matthew 1:22).

In my forty-plus years as an institute teacher, I was pleased to see many young adults come back to an institute class and start the process of regaining activity in the Church after several years of wandering on forbidden paths, looking for good times in the great and spacious building. They've told me of their experiences of being swept away in the river of filth running next to the floating building. They spoke of addictions and slavery to their passions and the difficulty of the long road back.

Their fall from grace was seldom a sudden one-time event. They hardly ever woke up one day and said, "I think I'll try being a slave to Satan and see what happens." The deceiver is much too clever for that. Their fall came slowly, naturally, and with great ease. All they had to do was . . . nothing. It's easy to not go to college. It's easy not to set goals or take care of ourselves and put off forever being prepared for marriage and responsibility. Never-never land has no entrance requirements.

To be worthy of true love takes work. There are three admission requirements we all must strive for, and all of them involve striving for unity.

The First Great Unity: Unity with God

Proverbs tells us "the fear of the Lord is the beginning of wisdom" (Proverbs 9:10). Oneness with God begins by awakening to who we are by study, prayer, and learning about our Creator and Benefactor. The Prophet Joseph Smith taught in the *Lectures on Faith* that it was necessary to have "an acquaintance"[87] with the divine attributes of the Father and the Son to have faith in Them. When we discover who and what God is and the nature of our relationship to Him, we then—without compulsion or coercion—voluntarily commit to love Him with all our hearts, souls, and minds above all other possible competing interests. This is the first step in the first unity.

"Master, which is the great commandment in the law? Jesus said unto him, Thou shalt love the Lord thy God with all thy heart, and with all thy soul, and with all thy mind. This is the first and great commandment" (Mathew 22:36–38). In John 17:11, the Savior prayed for His beloved Apostles that they may be one with Him. "Holy Father, keep through thine own name those whom thou hast given me, that they may be one, as we are."

Jesus next prayed that all those who will believe on Him through the work of His Apostles might also become one with them as the Twelve are one with Him and as He is one with the Father. "Neither pray I for these alone, but for them also which shall believe on me through their word; that they all may be one; as thou, Father, art in me, and I in thee, that they also may be one in us: that the world may believe that thou hast sent me. And the glory which thou gavest me I have given them; that they may be one, even as we are one" (John 17: 20–22).

After learning what and who God is, we then commit to become one with our Savior in the same sense that Christ is one with the Father and with the Twelve Apostles. We seek not to become physically one with the Godhead, but rather one in character, thought, actions, and deeds in as much as it is possible for mortals with faith to achieve.

Satan is constantly tempting us through false educational ideas, the flattery of prominent people, and all forms of electronic media that the goal of unity with God is nothing compared to the glamor and glitz of the great and spacious building. Step one is to not be deceived or distracted and to seek this first great unity earnestly.

The Second Great Unity: Unity with Zion

The second unity is similar to the first in that after we commit to unity with God by developing His character traits and values, we next commit to help God in doing His work on earth. We do this by becoming one with the Apostles and prophets in helping to establish Zion and prepare the earth for the Savior's return. John explained this in the previous passage. Those who believe in Jesus through the word of the Apostles become united with them and help them to bring forth and establish Zion.

In Moses 7:18, the Lord defined Zion as a group of people that spiritually are of one heart and mind and who take care of each other temporally when the need arises: "And the Lord called his people Zion, because they were of one heart and one mind, and dwelt in righteousness; and there was no poor among them."

The Savior taught the importance of unity of the Saints in both the New Testament and the Book of Mormon:

- 1 Corinthians 1:10—"Now I beseech you, brethren, by the name of our Lord Jesus Christ, that ye all speak the same thing, and that there be no divisions among you; but that ye be perfectly joined together in the same mind and in the same judgment."
- Ephesians 4:13 (11–14)—"Till we all come in the unity of the faith, and of the knowledge of the Son of God, unto a perfect man, unto the measure of the stature of the fulness of Christ."
- 4 Nephi 1:17 (15–17)—"There were no robbers, nor murderers, neither were there Lamanites, nor any manner of -ites; but they were in one, the children of Christ, and heirs to the kingdom of God."
- 3 Nephi 11:28 (28–30)—"And according as I have commanded you thus shall ye baptize. And there shall be no disputations among you, as there have hitherto been; neither shall there be disputations among you concerning the points of my doctrine, as there have hitherto been."

Jesus Christ also emphasized the importance of unity in Zion in latter-day scriptures:

- Doctrine and Covenants 38:27—"Behold, this I have given unto you as a parable, and it is even as I am. I say unto you, be one; and if ye are not one ye are not mine."
- Doctrine and Covenants 38:37—"I say unto you, be one; and if ye are not one ye are not mine."
- Doctrine and Covenants 35:2—"I am Jesus Christ, the Son of God, who was crucified for the sins of the world, even as many as will believe on my name, that they may become the sons of

God, even one in me as I am one in the Father, as the Father is one in me, that we may be one."

The Third Great Unity: True Love and Eternal Marriage

This third unity has two parts. The first part is to learn to love mankind in general. It is the second great commandment: "And the second is like unto it, Thou shalt love thy neighbour as thyself. On these two commandments hang all the law and the prophets" (Matthew 22:39–40). My observation is that most women understand this commandment naturally and observe it from childhood. Most men need a full-time missionary-type experience to learn it completely. However we learn it, from our mother's example or from mission work or from our life's experiences, we need to love all mankind before we can expect to narrow that love and focus on an eternal companion and family.

The Apostle John worded it this way: "For he that loveth not his brother whom he hath seen, how can he love God whom he hath not seen?" (1 John 4:20). I do not believe it's possible to become one with God or an eternal companion if we cannot develop a love for all mankind. One of the signs of the times of the last days is a lack of this type of love. "And the love of men shall wax cold, and iniquity shall abound" (D&C 45:27). Notice also the connection between the love of men waxing cold and the iniquity of wandering on forbidden paths.

After achieving unity with God and His Church and the love of mankind (part one), then we are ready for part two. However, Satan works extremely hard to keep couples from finding the third unity and going to the temple and entering into the new and everlasting covenant of marriage. Satan knows when we do this, it gives us protection against him and his plans to enslave and destroy us. His anti-marriage message is carried in much of our modern music, movies, TV, concerts, books, magazines, and many higher education classes. His disinformation ad agency has an unlimited budget and comes straight at us every day.

So the Lord counters Satan's disinformation campaign with truth and the plan of salvation. Those who aren't deceived then begin the lifelong process of finding and maintaining pure love and striving for the most difficult unity of all: becoming one with a human being of the opposite sex.

President Ezra Taft Benson taught us what this type of oneness means: "A husband and wife must attain righteous unity and oneness in their goals, desires, and actions."[88] Goals, desires, and actions—sounds easy, right? It definitely is not, as there's nothing more strange (it seems at times) than the mind of someone of the opposite sex. Picture Rex Harrison in the movie *My Fair Lady*, singing the lyrics, "Why can't a woman be more like a man?" Harrison's movie character, Professor Henry Higgins, had spent his whole life as a bachelor, devoted only to his studies and personal interests. He had a lot to learn about women as he found himself totally confused by one.

Becoming one with an eternal mate is the heart of the plan of salvation. Doctrine and Covenants 49:16 goes so far as to teach that the entire reason for the creation of the earth is to provide a place and environment where a man and a woman can learn to become one and, in the process, achieve a godlike stature: "Wherefore, it is lawful that he should have one wife, and they twain shall be one flesh, and all this that the earth might answer the end of its creation."

The scriptures make it clear what will happen when the time comes for the Savior's return if there are not couples sealed together for time and all eternity with their families and their posterities linked together in unity. This needs to happen in all the nations of the earth. If it does not happen, all four standard works state that the earth will be smitten with a curse and utterly wasted. Doctrine and Covenants 2:3: "If it were not so, the whole earth would be utterly wasted at his coming." (See also Joseph Smith—History 1:39; Malachi 4:6; Luke 1:17; and 3 Nephi 25:6.)

The earth was created to provide a place that we would be sent to achieve our divine destiny by becoming one with God and His Zion, getting married for time and all eternity, and then rearing children in righteousness. To fail to do so *when we had the opportunity* is to waste our mortal probationary period and fail the final exam.

It's not hard to understand why Satan works so hard to redefine the institution of covenant marriage into something different from God's plan for man. Satan's plan teaches a counterfeit form of love that creates unions that have neither the desire nor sometimes the ability to create children, nor even the motivation to provide a stable environment for them if couples do have them. Neither homosexual unions nor unmarried cohabitation unions have the potential to exalt those that participate in them and move them toward becoming one with God. They are fruitless unions.

The Church seeks not to punish those who choose to deviate from God's plan. The punishment is self-inflicted by the participants themselves. Sometimes there are natural consequences that come from the unnatural behaviors associated with these deviations from the Lord's path. However, the greatest consequence is simply the loss of promised blessings and divine destiny.

The reason for this is taught plainly in Doctrine and Covenants 131:1–4: "In the celestial glory there are three heavens or degrees; and in order to obtain the highest, a man must enter into this order of the priesthood [meaning the new and everlasting covenant of marriage]; and if he does not, he cannot obtain it. He may enter into the other, but that is the end of his kingdom; he cannot have an increase."

Brigham Young taught, "The new and everlasting covenant of marriage lays the foundation for eternal life. It [eternal marriage] is without beginning of days or end of years. We can tell some things with regard to it; it lays the foundation for worlds, for angels, and for the Gods; for intelligent beings to be crowned with glory, immortality, and eternal lives."[89]

Every doctrine and program of the Church points us toward the new and everlasting covenant of marriage. The entire plan of salvation points individuals in the direction of finding an eternal mate and learning to become one with them. Everything Satan does is designed to make us forget who we are, what we can become, and what it takes to qualify as heirs in God's kingdom.

President Joseph Fielding Smith said,

> The new and everlasting covenant . . . is everything—the fulness of the gospel. So marriage properly performed, baptism, ordination to the priesthood, everything else—every contract, every obligation, every performance that pertains to the gospel of Jesus Christ, which is sealed by the Holy Spirit of promise according to his law . . . is a part of the new and everlasting covenant. Therefore, all who seek a place in the kingdom of God are under the obligation and commandment to

abide in the new and everlasting covenant, which is the fullness of the gospel with all its rites, covenants, gifts, and obligations, or they "shall be damned, saith the Lord" (D&C 132:6).[90]

The Ultimate Marriage Goal and Blessing: Calling and Election

Elder Bruce R. McConkie explained the relationship between the doctrine of calling and election and eternal marriage:

> This may sound like a hard and difficult subject. It is one which is not fully known or understood by everyone, but easily understood doctrine. There is nothing complex or mysterious about it. Rather it is a doctrine we should understand.
>
> Thus, making one's calling and election sure grows out of baptism for one thing, and it grows out of celestial marriage for another. There is no such thing as gaining exaltation and eternal life except in and through the continuation of the family unit in eternity. Since making one's calling and election sure grows out of celestial marriage, the Lord took occasion to reveal the doctrine relative to it in connection with the revelation on marriage. If we enter in at this gate of marriage and then pursue a steadfast course, we gain eternal life.
>
> Making our calling and election sure is thus a matter of being married in the temple and of keeping the terms and conditions of the new and everlasting covenant of marriage. After entering in at the gate of celestial marriage, if we keep the commandments, then at some subsequent time, after great devotion and righteousness, after the Lord has proved us at all hazards, then he says, "Ye shall come forth in the first resurrection . . . and shall inherit thrones, kingdoms, principalities, and powers, dominions, all heights and depths" (D&C 132:19).
>
> In other words God, by revelation, tells us that our calling and election is made sure, that we are sealed up unto eternal life.[91]

The Ideal and the Reality

The ideal and the reality of each of our situations may not always come together in perfect harmony. It may well have to do with the nature of our second estate testing period. We know that our loving Creator designed each individual's final mortal exam especially for him or her. We can't always see the purpose in our trials at first, but we do know God sometimes gives us weaknesses to make us strong.

Paul put it this way: "And not only so, but we glory in tribulations also: knowing that tribulation worketh patience; And patience, experience; and experience, hope: and hope maketh not ashamed; because the love of God is shed abroad in our hearts by the Holy Ghost which is given unto us" (Romans 5:2–5; see also Ether 12:27).

The sequence seems to be we are given tribulations that lead us to learn patience. From our patience, we gain experience. Then, given enough experiences, we learn to cope with about anything, which gives us hope, optimism, and great faith. We come to understand that God's love includes giving us the obstacles to be overcome and the gift of the Holy Ghost to defeat them with.

I know many righteous single women and a few men who have achieved the first, second, and half of the third unity discussed in this appendix perfectly, but through circumstances uniquely personal to each of them, they don't have an eternal companion to complete the third unity with.

Sometimes married couples don't have the opportunity to perfect their third unity through no fault of their own. One woman married in her thirties, had a child, and lost her husband in a car wreck before the end of the first year of marriage. Another lost her husband to illness after twenty-five years of marriage and ten children, and she bravely carries on alone. Another didn't find her true love until she was fifty-five and does well in making up for lost time.

Others are older than fifty-five and still waiting for a third unity mate. Still others lose eternal mates in middle age to divorce because of their partner's poor choices and they are successfully fighting to carry on with their lives and stay positive. In each case, the Alvin Principle applies (see page XIV), and President Lorenzo Snow's counsel should give us confidence and hope: "There is no Latter-day Saint who dies after having lived a faithful life who will lose anything because of having failed to do certain things when opportunities were not furnished him or her."[92]

Endnotes

1. *Teachings of the Prophet Joseph Smith*, sel. Joseph Fielding Smith (1976), 255–56.

2. *The Teachings of Lorenzo Snow*, comp. Clyde J. Williams (Salt Lake City: Bookcraft, 1984), 138.

3. Gordon B. Hinckley, "A Conversation with Single Adults," *Ensign*, March 1997.

4. Neal A. Maxwell, "Enlightened by the Spirit of Truth," in *Men and Women of Christ*, 24.

5. Quoted by John Taylor, in "The Organization of the Church," *Millennial Star*, November 15, 1851, 339.

6. See Dallin H. Oaks, "Stand as a Witness of God," *Ensign*, March 2015, 29.

7. Joseph B. Wirthlin, "Our Lord and Savior," *Ensign*, November 1993, 5.

8. John A. Widtsoe, *Evidences and Reconciliations* (Salt Lake City: Bookcraft, 1987), 297.

9. Wesley Burr, Brenton Yorgason, and Terry Baker, *Creating a Celestial Marriage* (Bookcraft: Salt Lake City, 1982), 127.

10. For more information on the nature of prayer, see the Bible Dictionary, "Prayer."

11. CES Fireside, Brigham Young University, Provo, Utah, January 9, 1994.

12. Abraham Maslow, *The Farther Reaches of Human Nature* (New York: Penguin, October 1993).

13. *Responding to Abuse: Helps for Ecclesiastical Leaders* (Salt Lake City: The Church of Jesus Christ of Latter-day Saints), page 1.

14. James E. Faust, "Father, Come Home," *Ensign*, May 1993.

15. Dell Van Orden, "Hinckleys to Note 60th Anniversary," *Church News*, April 19, 1997, 3.

16. Gordon B. Hinckley, *Cornerstones of a Happy Home* (pamphlet, 1984), 4–5.

17. Kings 5.

18. Gordon B. Hinckley, "Forgiveness," *Ensign,* October 2005.

19. See Terry R. Baker, "How Gospel Truths Enhance Self-Esteem in Marriage," *Ensign*, July 1984.

20. Henry Fink, *Romantic Love and Personal Beauty* (New York: Macmillan and Company, 1887).

21. Paul Tillich, *Dynamics of Faith* (New York: Harper and Row, 1957), 114–15.

22. Gordon B. Hinckley (Anchorage, Alaska, regional conference, June 18, 1995).

23. Eric Fromm, *The Art of Loving* (New York: Harper and Row, 1956), 45–46.

24. Ibid.

25. Spencer W. Kimball, *Teachings of Spencer W. Kimball*, ed. Edward L. Kimball (Salt Lake City: Bookcraft, 1995), 279.

26. Boyd K. Packer, *Eternal Love* (Salt Lake City: Deseret Book, 1973), 15.

27. Sara Israelsen-Hartley, "Y. study: Premarital sex to ensure 'compatibility' potentially harmful," *Deseret News*, December 21, 2010.

28. Daniel Goldstein, et al., *The Dance-Away Lover: And Other Roles We Play in Love, Sex, and Marriage* (New York: Morrow, 1977).

29. In Conference Report, September–October 1955, 13.

30. Robert Sternburg, "A Triangular Theory of Love," *Psychological Review* (93), 1986, 119–135.

31. Wesley Burr, Brenton Yorgason, and Terry Baker, *Creating a Celestial Marriage*, 127–29.

32. Dallin H. Oaks, "Divorce," *Ensign*, May 2007, 70–73.

33. Gordon B. Hinckley, "Our Fading Civility," Brigham Young University, commencement and inauguration ceremony, April 25, 1996.

34. Laura Betzig, "Causes of Conjugal Dissolution: A Cross-Cultural Study," *Current Anthropology* 30(5), 1989, 654–76.

35. Paul R. Amato and Stacy J. Rogers, "A Longitudinal Study of Marital Problems and Subsequent Divorce," *Journal of Marriage and the Family* 59(3), 1997, 612–24.

36. Graham B. Spanier and Randie L. Margolis, "Marital Separation and Extramarital Sexual Behavior," *Journal of Sex Research* 19(1), 1983, 23–48.

37. Michael W. Wiederman, "Extramarital Sex: Prevalence and Correlates in a National Survey," *Journal of Sex Research* 34(2), 1997, 167–74.

38. Shirley P. Glass and Thomas L. Wright, "Justifications for Extramarital Relationships: The Association between Attitudes, Behaviors, and Gender," *Journal of Sex Research* 29(3), 1992, 361–87.

39. Judith Treas and Deirdre Giesen, "Sexual Infidelity Among Married and Cohabiting Americans," *Journal of Marriage and the Family* 62(1), 2000, 48–60.

40. David C. Atkins, Donald H. Baucom, and Neil S. Jacobson, "Understanding Infidelity: Correlates in a National Random Sample," *Journal of Family Psychology* 15(4), 2001, 735–49.

41. Dallin H. Oaks, *Pure in Heart* (Salt Lake City: Bookcraft, June 1988), 75–76.

42. Merriam-Webster Dictionary, "Pride."

43. Ezra Taft Benson, "Beware of Pride," *Ensign*, May 1989, 4–7.

44. Ibid.

45. John Gottman, *Why Marriages Succeed or Fail: And How You Can Make Yours Last* (New York: Simon & Schuster, 1994), 69.

46. Ibid., 68.

47. Spencer W. Kimball, "Oneness in Marriage," *Ensign*, March 1977.

48. Pew Research Center Publications, "The Decline of Marriage and Rise of New Families," November 18, 2010; see also the National Marriage Project, "The State of Our Unions," Marriage in America 2009.

49. The National Marriage Project, "The State of Our Unions," Marriage in America 1999, ix.

50. The National Marriage Project, "The State of Our Unions," Marriage in America 2002, 5.

51. "The Family: A Proclamation to the World," *Ensign*, November 1995, 102.

52. Frank D. Cox, *Human Intimacy: Marriage, the Family, and Its Meaning*, Tenth Edition (Wadsworth Group, 2009), 29.

53. See "Entropy" on Wikipedia.

54. See John Gottman, *Why Marriages Succeed or Fail*, 55–66.

55. See Ibid., 103–136.

56. Gordon B. Hinckley, (Anchorage, Alaska, regional conference, 18 June 1995).

57. Aileen H. Clyde, "'Charity Suffereth Long,'" *Ensign*, November 1991, 77.

58. Henry B. Eyring, "Safety in Counsel," *Ensign,* June 2008.

59. Spencer W. Kimball, *The Teachings of Spencer W. Kimball,* 327.

60. Ibid., 329.

61. Ezra Taft Benson, "To the Mothers in Zion" (fireside for parents, February 22, 1987), 8.

62. "To the Elect Women of the Kingdom of God," Nauvoo Illinois Relief Society Dedication, June 30, 1978; See also Ezra Taft Benson, *Teachings of Ezra Taft Benson,* 506–7, 548–49.

63. Ezra Taft Benson, "The Honored Place of Woman," *Ensign,* November 1981, 105.

64. Ezra Taft Benson, "In His Steps," in *Speeches of the Year,* May 4, 1979, 64.

65. In Conference Report, October 1970, 24.

66. Howard W. Hunter, "Being a Righteous Husband and Father," *Ensign,* November 1994, 49–51.

67. Gordon B. Hinckley, "Walking in the Light of the Lord," *Ensign,* November 1998, 99–100.

68. Gordon B. Hinckley, "Women of the Church, *Ensign,* November 1996, 69.

69. Gordon B. Hinckley, "Live Up to Your Inheritance," *Ensign,* November 1983, 83.

70. Richard G. Scott, "The Power of Correct Principles," *Ensign,* May 1993, 34.

71. Frank D. Cox, *Human Intimacy: Marriage, the Family, and Its Meaning,* Eighth Edition (1999), chapter eight.

72. Gordon B. Hinckley, "Great Shall Be the Peace of Thy Children," *Ensign*, November 2000, 50–53.

73. Howard W. Hunter, "Prepare for Honorable Employment," *Ensign*, November 1975, 124.

74. Charles Francis Adams, *Diary of Charles Francis Adams*, ed. Aida DiPace Donald, Vol. 1 (Belknap Press, 1964), 350.

75. William Wordsworth, "Ode: Intimations of Immortality from Recollections of Early Childhood," *The Complete Poetical Works of William Wordsworth* (1924), 359.

76. *Demographic Winter: the decline of the human family.* Documentary produced by SRB Documentary and Acuity Productions Film. Produced by Barry Mclerran and Rick Stout, 2008.

77. "The Family: A Proclamation to the World," *Ensign*, November 1995, 102.

78. *Messages of the First Presidency*, comp. James R. Clark, Vol. 5 (Salt Lake City: Deseret Book), 244.

79. Gordon B. Hinckley, "The Light within You," *Ensign,* May 1995, 99.

80. Easton's Bible Dictionary, "Divine Destiny."

81. Brigham Young, *Discourses of Brigham Young*, comp. John A. Widtsoe (Salt Lake City: Deseret Book, 1954), 5.

82. Orson Pratt, "Celestial Marriage," *The Seer,* October 1853, 156.

83. James E. Faust, "A Growing Testimony," *Ensign*, November 2000, 53–54, 59.

84. Jonathan Jacobs, "An Eastern Orthodox Conception of Theosis and Human Nature," *Faith and Philosophy* 26(5), 2009.

85. "Lesson 16: Wilford Woodruff: Righteousness and the Protection of the Lord," *The Presidents of the Church: Teacher's Manual* (Salt Lake City: The Church of Jesus Chirst of Latter-day Saints), 74.

86. James E. Faust, "The Forces That Will Save Us," *Ensign*, January 2007.

87. Joseph Smith Jr., *Lectures on Faith* (1985), 42.

88. In Conference Report, October 1982, 85.

89. *Teachings of Presidents of the Church: Brigham Young* (Salt Lake City: The Church of Jesus Christ of Latter-day Saints).

90. Joseph Fielding Smith, *Doctrines of Salvation,* comp. Bruce R. McConkie, 3 vols. (1954–56), 1:158.

91. Bruce R. McConkie, "Making Our Calling and Election Sure," in *Speeches of the Year*, March 25, 1969.

92. *The Teachings of Lorenzo Snow*, comp. Clyde J. Williams (Salt Lake City: Bookcraft, 1984), 138.

About the Author

Terry R. Baker and his wife, Patty, have been married since 1965. They have eight children and over twenty grandchildren. Dr. Baker has a PhD from Brigham Young University in family studies and marriage and family counseling. He taught seminary and institute for the Church for over forty years in California, Texas, and most recently Utah. He was an adjunct professor teaching marriage and family classes at BYU for fifteen years. He served our country as a National Guard chaplain for thirty years in North Carolina, Texas, Missouri, Utah, California, and Vietnam. Dr. Baker coauthored four previous books on marriage, published three *Ensign* articles, and wrote dating, courtship, and marriage institute manuals for the Church Education System. Dr. Baker served a mission in Southern Australia in 1963–64, and he and Patty served a senior mission in San Diego, California, in 2014–15.